Hollins College: An Illustrated History

Hollins College
An Illustrated History

Frances J. Niederer

The University Press of Virginia

Charlottesville

THE UNIVERSITY PRESS OF VIRGINIA
Copyright © 1973 by the Rector and Visitors
of the University of Virginia

First published 1973

ISBN: 0-8139-0472-2
Library of Congress Catalog Card Number: 72–97863
Printed in the United States of America

Foreword

ORIGINALLY I projected this book as a pictorial history, with the hope that photographs might capture the individuality retained by the Hollins milieu through the century and a half since its founding and might reflect those activities in which generations of students have participated. But pictures proved inadequate to describe the intellectual concerns for which the milieu was developed, and many facts and figures seemed worthy of inclusion as matters of record. The pattern of the book then changed to become perhaps unorthodox, being neither pictorial history nor history with illustrations. Introductory remarks, brief for the early period, inevitably expanded as Hollins itself grew and became more complex. The assembling of illustrations in groups still seemed to be logical; so I placed them after the text for each chapter. The reader may choose: either word or image may come first. And if she wishes, the alumna may begin with her own generation at Hollins, turning backward or looking forward to note continuity and change.

I have taken the successive campus quadrangles and the buildings that define them to delineate frames for intellectual and social activities. In the early years, almost all students and staff members participated in these activities, and they have all been included. For later years, a choice had to be made. I decided to stress those that grew into traditions and also those of which the majority of students were aware, even if individuals did not participate in them. Much more difficult were the choices that had to be made among the men and women whose personalities and influence were vital to the establishment and growth of Hollins College, and only reluctantly did I decide against identifying every person appearing in each picture. I realize that many readers will miss cherished people and events, but I hope that memories may be reinforced by what is included. I find reassuring the comment from a current Hollins senior: "After all, we have our annuals."

Many colleagues and friends aided in the preparation of this book, and encouragement came from many alumnae and students; it is impossible to acknowledge my indebtedness to all of them. There are several, however, who must be mentioned. Archivists Margaret P. Scott and Rachel Wilson have for years painstakingly collected documents and identified and dated pictures; they made all freely available to me. Shirley Henn cheerfully contributed editorial advice and an alumna's point of view during her reading of the manuscript. Willard N. James not only read it but kindly refrained from pointing out that much of the text from 1950 on simply paraphrases his articles in the *Hollins Herald* and utilizes many of his photographs. Virginia L. Carter, Director of Information and Publications, should be considered a coauthor, both for her willing, continuous advice and for her supplying innumerable photographs. President John A. Logan, Jr., generously read the last chapter and gave helpful suggestions. To all of these I am most grateful.

The task of covering material in the Hollins archives was made much easier by the solid and selective groundwork of many earlier publications. Notable among these are the article by Joseph A. Turner and Robert M. Hughes entitled "Roanoke Female Seminary, Valley Union Seminary, Hollins Institute, and Hollins College," *William and Mary College Quarterly* (October 1929); Dorothy Scovil Vickery's *Hollins College, 1842–1942: an Historical Sketch* (1942); Anne M. Montgomery's "Hollins College," *The Iron Worker* (winter, 1954–55); and President John A. Logan's address entitled "Hollins: An Act of Faith for 125 Years," delivered at a Newcomen Society Dinner honoring Hollins's 125th anniversary and later published in the *Hollins College Bulletin* (February 1968). Other sources are mentioned throughout the text. Fortunately, members of the Hollins community have always been prolific writers and eager photographers, and alumnae have liberally contributed to the archives everything from honorary medals to personal memory albums.

Grants from the Ford Foundation and Hollins College aided in securing photographs and in the preparation of the text. I am grateful for this assistance, as I am also to Bob Crawford for his meticulous copying of old photographs and making of new ones.

Hollins College   F.J.N.
May 1972

Contents

Hollins College: An Illustrated History

CHARLES JOHNSTON (Fig. 1) Charles Johnston from Lynchburg, merchant, hotel owner, and author, had traveled into the wilderness of Kentucky in 1790. In 1829 Harper's published his *Narrative,* an account of his capture on the Ohio River by Indians and his ransom at Sandusky, an Indian trading post, by the French trader Francis Duchouquet, who later visited him at Botetourt Springs. (The names of Sandusky and Duchouquet were later to be given to houses on the Hollins College campus.)

Latrobe in 1832 judged Johnston to be a man "whose fortunes are reduced to his present occupation, without his feelings or habits being altered with the circumstances," commenting, "he still sits at the head of his long table, with an air, and his daughter sits at the foot. The conduct of the guests here is corresponding, and there is more general politeness here than is to be met with often at these Virginia watering places."

I. Prelude

Botetourt Springs and the Roanoke Female Seminary, 1820—1841

THE history of Hollins College begins with the hotel and cottages built near mineral springs in a wooded hollow below Tinker Mountain. Charles Johnston, seeing in the site attractive possibilities for one of those popular spas being established throughout southwestern Virginia, built here about 1820 a hotel that he called Botetourt Springs, after the county in which his land lay. This county, formed in 1770, had been named for Lord Botetourt, then colonial governor of Virginia. Johnston's land, a tract of 475 acres, was part of the 900 acres originally given to the pioneer Welshman, William Carvin, as a royal grant from King George II in 1746. Remains of Carvin's fortified log house stood on a rise north of the springs.

In the hollow Johnston placed a hotel and cottages, in an open quadrangle oriented toward Tinker Mountain, whose distinctive silhouette formed a bar across the valley between the low ranges of the Allegheny and the Blue Ridge mountains. About a mile and a half northwest lay Carvin's Cove with its picturesque waterfall, from which Carvin's Creek flowed through the hotel grounds.

Patronage for the new resort was in part assured by its location close to the turnpike that led west to Tennessee and northeast to Washington. This old road, long since gone, ran through the present site of Main Building, crossed Carvin's Creek a few feet from the sulphur spring, and continued over the hill to the southwest. According to the advertisement placed in the Richmond *Constitutional Whig* by Johnston in 1825, "the western mail-stage from Richmond passing through Lynchburg will come directly to this place. Such gentlemen as do not wish to be encumbered with horses and carriages, can adopt that mode of conveyance."

Among the guests known to have visited Botetourt Springs were Andrew Jackson, Henry Clay, and, happily for the notes and sketches he made on the spot, John H. B. Latrobe of Baltimore, who had followed the daughter of General Leigh Claiborne to court her here.

Charles Johnston operated the resort until his death in 1833. It was then taken over and run by Hezekiah Daggs, who also owned the watering place at Hot Springs, which was to prosper. But the popularity of Botetourt was on the wane. In 1839 it was closed, and the property and buildings were put up for sale.

Both were taken over that same year by Edward William Johnston, nephew of Charles, who transferred to the site the school he had been running in Liberty (now Bedford), Virginia. He took for it the name of the county of Roanoke, newly chartered in 1838. The Roanoke Female Seminary at Botetourt Springs, short-lived though it was, marked the transition from watering place to educational institution. Unfortunately it never flourished—indeed, it drew barely a dozen or so students; no changes were made in buildings or grounds. By 1842 the property, debt-ridden and run down, was again on the market.

Some pictures of the seminary staff and students, reports, and letters remain, however, notably those written by Eliza Johnston, spirited niece of the headmaster, to her mother in Burke's Garden and to her brother in West Point. Reports indicate classes in reading, writing, spelling, arithmetic, history, music, and French. Eliza mentions a birthday party for Mrs. Johnston at "the great house," with terrapin and cherry pie, and speaks of the girls "fixing little flower beds before our cabin doors." Elizabeth Steptoe in 1838 writes of their bathing in the creek and of "a delightful party here on the 1st day of May, which day is generally celebrated with great rejoicings in nearly all female schools."

SPRINGS (Figs. 2, 3) Latrobe's watercolor sketch of the sulphur spring shows the high rail fences on the property and a log cabin in the background. Of the spring he wrote: "The quality of the water is the same as the White Sulphur water, although in a lesser degree." Charles L. Cocke on his arrival in 1846 was to write to his father that "one may smell the water at times from 30 to 40 yards off."

There were other springs on the grounds, the chief limestone spring (with "free-stone" water, good for drinking) being at the corner between the present West and Main buildings. Its springhouse, built of limestone blocks with hand-hewn roof timbers, is held to be the spring of William Carvin and the oldest structure on the Hollins campus.

"To promote the effects of each," Johnston advertised, "hot, cold, and shower baths are provided." Later Hollins Institute catalogues were to add chalybeate to the beneficial minerals found in the waters. And from 1902 to 1917, catalogues published the results of analysis of the water of the sulphur spring by the Federal Health Department; these reported the water "pure and wholesome," with high percentages of calcium bicarbonate, magnesium sulphate, and chlorine.

I & F Winkler Des

BOTETOURT SPRINGS HOTEL (Fig. 4) Although this lithograph was published in 1853, decades after the hotel was erected, it gives us a good idea of Charles Johnston's establishment, for the only additions are the small wings, shown at each side of the "big house," that were added in 1849. The main structure was a two-storied brick building, which until 1900 served as the central section of the present West Building. At right angles to its ends, running in front of the sites of the present Main and Administration buildings, were one-storied brick cottages, seven in all, of two to four rooms each. These cottages housed pupils, faculty, or guests of the subsequent schools through the 1850s. The turnpike was directly behind the cottages shown on the right.

MANTEL (Fig. 5) Reset in the small sitting room of the present Main Building is this mantel from the parlor of the hotel. The delicate Adam detail of the woodwork indicates that the hotel parlor had some handsome touches. Here, said Johnston, "music of the best kind will be provided for Dancing, and such as are fond of playing on the Forte-Piano will find in the drawing-room an elegant one provided for their use."

WITCH DOOR (Fig. 6) The north basement door of the present West Building is an original one saved from the hotel of 1820. It bears the double-cross design which, in popular belief, warded off evil spirits. Some small-paned windows in the rear of West are also of this early date.

TINKER MOUNTAIN (Fig. 7) "At Botetourt the Tinker Mountains terminate in front of the house," wrote Latrobe, and as part of his courting he "aided the footsteps of the fair Miss Claiborne" to the summit, about a thousand feet above the grounds. According to strongest tradition, the mountain is named after a tinker (or tinkers) who worked either on the mountain or along the creek at its base during the Revolutionary period. But F. B. Kegley, eminent historian of southwestern Virginia, remarked that Tinker is a variant of the name Tencher, and suggested that since Tenchers lived in the vicinity, both creek and mountain may have been named for them.

One assumes (thinking of decades of wood-burning fireplaces) that more heavily wooded areas existed then than now remain. Yet Latrobe wrote: "the country around is open, and the mountains that rise in all directions do not press upon you so closely as other places I have visited in Virginia." Johnston recommended hunting to his patrons, "the adjacent mountains abounding in game." Mrs. Charles Lewis Cocke was three times to see a bear cross the school grounds, and Nannie Armistead's diary of 1866 often mentions that classes were suspended because professors had gone hunting.

Between Botetourt Springs and the mountain rose the low rounded hill of Little Tinker, a favorite place for rural walks and horseback rides until it was cut through by U.S. Route 81 in the 1960s.

Edward William Johnston
1840

Monsieur Villegrande

Germain Bedaette

Madame Villegrande

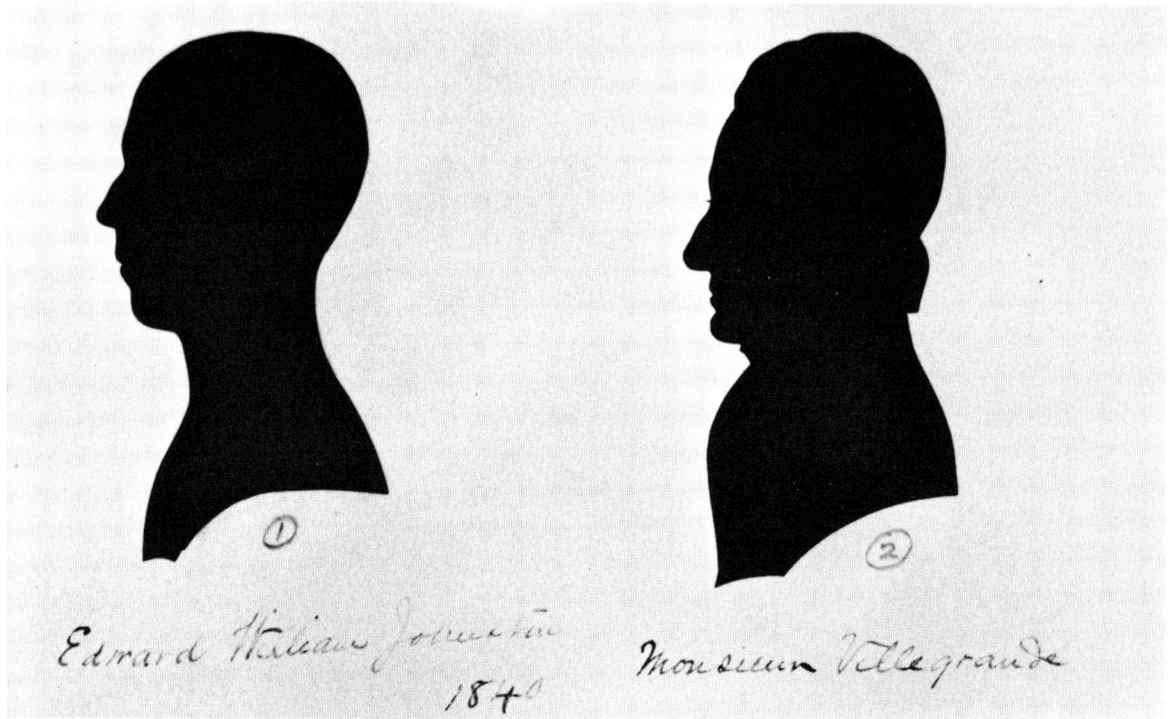

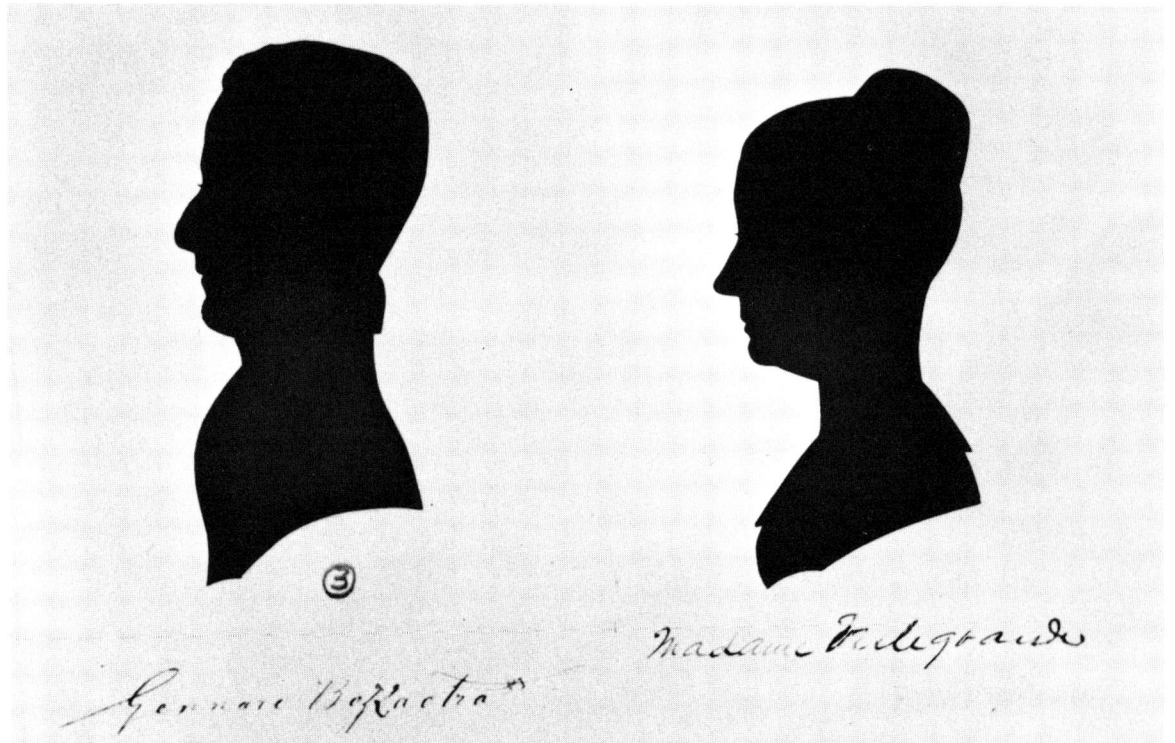

8. Silhouettes of seminary staff

6

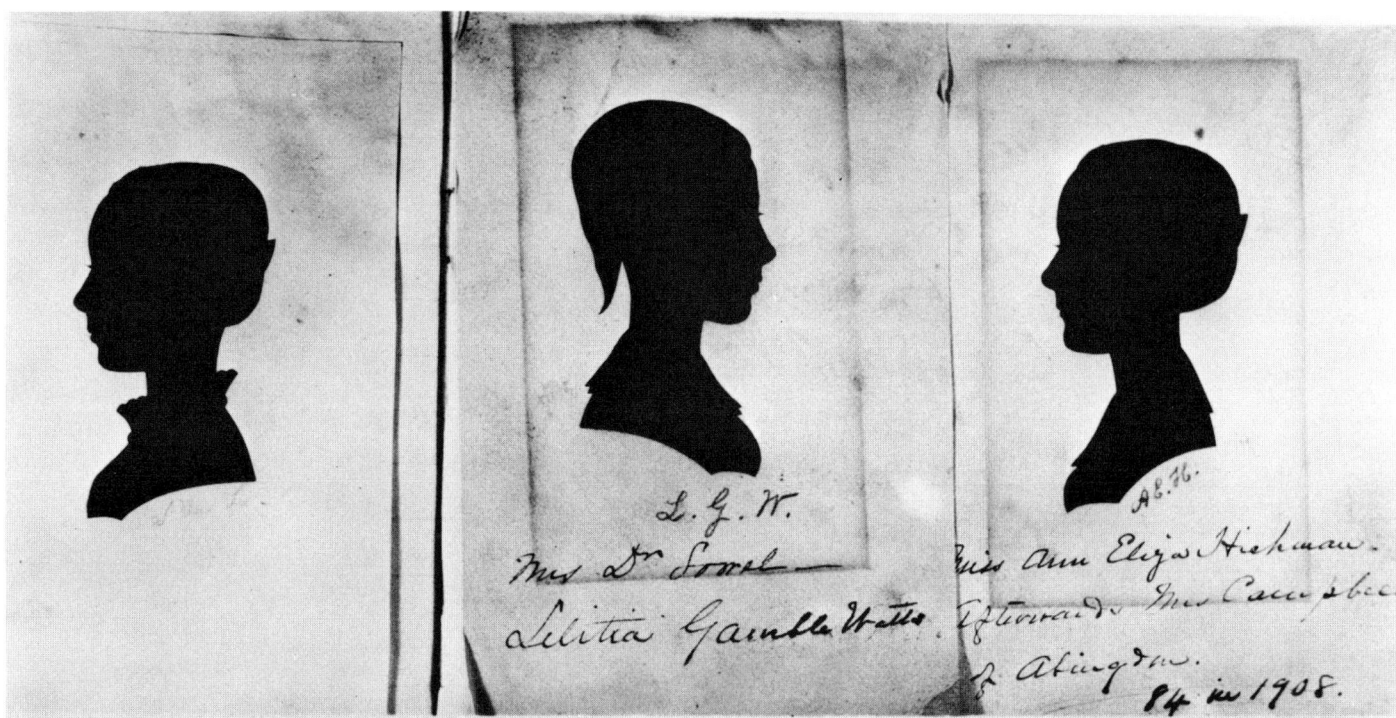

SEMINARY STUDENTS, 1840 (Fig. 9) Girls were required to wear bottle-green Circassian or Merino dresses with capes and cane or straw bonnets (Nun's pattern) trimmed with crimson ribbons. Demerits were given for walking outdoors without bonnets.

STAFF OF THE ROANOKE FEMALE SEMINARY, 1840 (Fig. 8) Pictured in silhouettes from left to right are Edward Johnston, M. Villegrande, Gennaio Bozkaotra, and Mme. Villegrande. M. Villegrande taught French; Eliza Johnston wrote to her brother that she had "some very dreadful news. . . . I have to take my meals down at the other house for the purpose of talking French." The Italian Bozkaotra taught piano and guitar. In 1840 a new dancing master, Mr. Goodsicki, arrived; the girls were enchanted with the romanticism of having a Polish exile. "Waltzes, Galopades, etc., he does to perfection. . . . We rise every morning at four to take a dancing lesson, and dance until six," wrote Eliza. (The rising bell was still being rung at four in 1863, as Betty Jane Miller noted in a letter written in June.)

THE CASCADE AT CARVIN'S COVE (Fig. 10) "I must tell you of the splendid picnic we had here last Saturday," wrote Eliza Johnston in 1840 to her brother at West Point. "Among other things that were sent from here Uncle Edward made up several bottles of Mint Julep without putting in any water, intending that to be added when they got there; this was neglected however, and the girls getting hold of it each took a pretty good pull at it. They were all pretty soon very merry, and one of them . . . was so affected that she fell into a swoon, and was brought home in a carpet by some of the gentlemen that were there. We are all in great consternation for fear that some horrible story will get out about it."

II. Founding and Early Years

The Valley Union Seminary and the Female Seminary at Botetourt Springs, 1842–1855

IN 1842, Joshua Bradley, a Baptist minister from the State of New York, purchased with deferred payment the property of the defunct Roanoke Female Seminary. "He then," wrote Charles Lewis Cocke later, "with the argument of large numbers and bright prospects, went to the people for money to pay for the property. His plan was to form an Education Society under the imposing title of 'The Valley Union Education Society of Virginia' [Fig. 11]. This

society was chartered on the principle of a joint-stock company, and was to conduct an institution for all denominations." The word *Union* in the title connoted this non-sectarian foundation; the *Valley* was the great Valley of Virginia.

Bradley was sufficiently persuasive to have the society formed by May 1843, with each member contributing at least fifty dollars, and the Reverend A. C. Dempsey serving as president. In January 1844, a charter was received from the General Assembly of Virginia. Colonel Tayloe, the society's first secretary-treasurer, then became president of the board of thirteen trustees. Succeeding him as president were the Reverends James Leftwich (1849–53), J. L. Prichard (1853–55), and James C. Clopton (1855–56), but then Tayloe was reelected and given a lifetime tenure.

Under Bradley's direction the school did not go well. Sufficient money was not forthcoming; he had trouble with

faculty—having, in 1843, only two beside himself—and, according to Cocke, also finding himself, "at his age of life, totally unqualified to manage Virginia youths, especially the more high-spirited." So in 1845 the Reverend Mr. Bradley moved on to Missouri. The trustees then took over the property (by now reduced to 106 acres) and looked for someone to run the school. Obviously what they needed was someone younger, able to act both as principal and business manager, and with some money to invest. They found their man in twenty-six-year-old Charles Lewis Cocke, business manager and teacher of mathematics at Richmond College, who had saved $1,500. Furthermore, he was complimented by their invitation and willing to accept as salary part of the fees he was to collect for tuition. He was to begin on July 1, 1846, with seventeen students and a faculty of three in addition to himself.

Charles Lewis Cocke, born February 21, 1820, at Edgehill in King William County, had attended Richmond College from 1836 to 1838 and continued at Columbian College (now George Washington University), graduating there in 1840. He then returned to Richmond College and at the close of the year married Susanna Pleasants. When the call came from the Valley Union Seminary the young Cockes had three children, and faced a five-day journey westward. With that accomplished by June 18, they settled and prepared for the opening of the session.

"Miss Susanna" took care of domestic matters—no easy task. She remarked later that "for a long time all our household supplies had to be brought up to Buchanan from Richmond by the canal-boat and wagoned 45 miles to Hollins." Charles Lewis did everything else. They had the full cooperation of the board of trustees, who also became increasingly indebted to the new principal because he spent so much of his putative salary on repairs and replenishments. Even his original investment of $1,500 had not been repaid by the end of the century.

There were many problems, physical, educational, and

continually economic; nevertheless the school grew. By the session 1846–47 when the first catalogue was published, there were 63 pupils—36 boys and 27 girls. What was expected of them was made clear in this first catalogue, and repeated for fifteen years: "This institution is not designed to be a resort for the pleasure-seeking, the idle, and the profligate, but shall be sacred to the cultivation of sound learning, virtuous feelings, and independent thought; and those who cannot join us with a determination to act in conformity with principles like these, would do far better for themselves, as well as for us, to remain away." In 1852, when the school was opened only to girls, the word *profligate* was changed to *gay* as more suitable to females. But even in the beginning, the sternness of the admonition was tempered by the statement about the faculty: "The officers of the institution will be expected to cultivate with the students habits of affection and familiar intercourse, and endeavour to influence them rather by appeals to their better feelings than by severe and disgraceful punishment."

The Valley Union Seminary admitted any candidates who possessed "correct moral habits, without distinction of religious views." By 1852–53 the catalogues were stating that "inculcation of sectarian principles" was "positively forbidden." (By the 1880s NOT SECTARIAN was being printed in capitals.) Ministers of varied denominations preached in the old hall of the seminary, and students were taken to Sabbath services in Salem and Fincastle. In 1855 a new Baptist church, Enon, was built across the highway on land granted by the Society; there students and staff attended both services and school functions such as commencement. Both Charles Lewis and Susanna Cocke were active in the Baptist church, and he was particularly involved in its charitable and educational movements, although keeping his own seminary nonsectarian.

By 1851–52 there were preparatory and collegiate departments at the seminary, handled by a faculty of seven. Classes had never been coeducational. Assistant teachers in the male department were housed with the boys in the cottages while the girls were in the "big house." Then in January 1851, a board resolution directed the principal to arrange "separate chapels and dining-rooms for the two departments." But the enrollment was too large for the accommodations, and it was decided to drop the male department.

Certainly, judging from the remaining books of demerits, there were fewer disciplinary problems with the boys gone. Some boys arrived with the strictly forbidden firearms or deadly weapons. They fought each other, sometimes with drawn knives; one shot a pistol on the way to a Dunkard meeting; they killed ducks or chickens to roast in their cottage fireplaces. They used intoxicating drink; they swore; they left chapel before the services ended. One after another was found "guilty of making an unusual noise at night" when blowing quills was in vogue, and they constantly "communicated with the Female Department." Some problems, at least, disappeared along with the coordinated school.

But Charles Lewis Cocke had written when he was just nineteen that he proposed to devote his life "to the higher education of women in the South." Boys were at first assigned a more demanding course of study, for they alone could rise to the fourth class, reading Tacitus and Thucydides. But by 1848 girls too were allowed to study Latin. Now in 1851, recommending to the board that the male department be abolished, Cocke advised that "the Female Department of a mixed school can never take a high stand as a Literary Institution . . . the necessary confinement of the Female Scholars is altogether incompatible with comfort and health." So in 1852 the seminary admitted women only, offering them a strong curriculum and "a mode of imparting instruction . . . well calculated to discipline the mind, and to give vigor and expansion to all its powers." The catalogue had a special paragraph recommending that young women be trained here for teaching.

The 1852–53 session of the Female Seminary at Botetourt Springs opened with 81 girls; by 1853–54 there were 150. Within the collegiate department varied courses were offered and students could elect to work for a diploma in one or more subjects: Latin, French, mathematics, physical science, music, or moral science (which, paralleling the University of Virginia's junior class scheme, included rhetoric, belles-lettres, and mental philosophy). A full graduate diploma, now offered, required the successful completion of five subjects plus a terminal essay on a literary or scientific subject. A single first full-graduate diploma was given in 1855 to Susan V. Williams of Farmville, Virginia.

Classes met from 8:00 A.M. to 4:00 P.M., with morning worship before breakfast and evening worship in the late afternoon. Students studied independently in their rooms, in the new French manner (although preparatory pupils still gathered in one large room to study under supervision). This practice cost the school more in heating, but was commendable since it followed progressive theory. Examinations lasted ten days, and perhaps then, as in the 1860s, each continued for eight or more hours. They were given in the presence of two faculty members and those parents or guardians who wished to attend.

Transportation to and from the seminary was becoming a bit easier than it had been in earlier years. In the late 1850s students could still come by the Valley Stage, alighting at Cloverdale, two miles distant. But they could also travel on the Virginia and Tennessee Railroad, which by 1852 had reached the area, with convenient stations at Bonsack's Depot and at Salem. In September 1853, the seminary acquired an omnibus drawn by a four-horse team to take students between stations and school at a fifty-cent fare. A new South Western turnpike, the "McAdamized Road," had been laid southeast of the school grounds (along present U.S. Route 11). In May 1852, the school received a hundred dollars for a piece of land sold for a tollhouse site at the point where the new road bridged Carvin's Creek.

There was constant repair and renovation of grounds and buildings through these years, notably enlargements of the old hall of Botetourt Springs Hotel. Upon his arrival, Cocke wrote later, "the numerous small buildings scattered over the grounds gave painful evidence of neglect and decay, the walkways were all obliterated by a luxuriant crop of grass and weeds." But with improvements and minor changes, the place served for fifteen years essentially as Charles Johnston had established it.

CHARLES LEWIS COCKE (Figs. 12, 13) Although Charles Lewis Cocke (1820–1901) came to the seminary two years after its establishment, he merits the title of founder later bestowed upon him, for without him the school would not have survived. Ledgers and reports witness the innumerable details he had to oversee, the constant small and large crises to be met. He planned curricula; he preached and gave countless addresses; he wrote constantly, often in an elegant style; he was interminably fund-raising. Varied notes by students attest their respect for his steadfast *in loco parentis* attitude, his concern for their health, their morals, their manners, and always and above all his insistence on their right to a stringent, disciplined education.

And he set up what was to develop into an academic dynasty at Botetourt Springs, for the school was decidedly a family affair. Five daughters and two sons worked under him, as did his brother and brother-in-law. Grandchildren continued the tradition, teaching or aiding in the administration of the successive schools on the site. So did relatives by marriage. Granddaughters, grandnieces, great-grands of all the various family branches were attending Hollins, also, in a network carrying on to the present day. Founder's Day, set in 1898 to commemorate Charles Lewis's birthday, long remained a large family party.

COLONEL GEORGE PLATER TAYLOE (Fig. 14) The struggling seminary owed much of its persistence and growth to the perspicacity and foresight of Colonel Tayloe (1804–1897), who served it for half a century in a lifetime tenure voted by the board. Through his parents, John Tayloe III, wealthy landowner of Richmond County, and Anne Ogle Tayloe, daughter of a governor of Maryland, he was early favored with the opportunities of an aristocratic milieu and introduced to a tradition of public service. He was further trained at Princeton and graduated in 1825.

After his marriage to Mary Elizabeth Langhorne in 1830, George Tayloe came to southwestern Virginia, settling finally in Roanoke on property acquired from his father-in-law. He took an active part in state politics, in community affairs, and in councils of the Episcopal church. To the Valley Union Education Society he gave valuable advice, considerable time, and frequent monetary aid. He was particularly astute in practical and legal matters, in which counsel was annually needed.

Surely Tayloe's taste and judgment must have played a key role in the growing handsomeness of buildings and grounds of the seminary and the later institute. He had been born in his grandfather's notable mansion, Mount Airy, and had grown up in his father's elegant Octagon House in Washington. Tayloe's Roanoke home, Buena Vista, is still an impressive structure.

15. The Female Seminary, 1854

THE FEMALE SEMINARY AT BOTETOURT SPRINGS (Fig. 15) Girls now occupied the fifty rooms available: thirty-one in the Main Building, nineteen in the cottages, some of which were now reserved for use as music rooms and as lodgings for visitors. Chapel and parlors were on the ground floor of the "big house," and a dining room in the basement, with a separate kitchen in back. If not luxurious, accommodations were still marked, as Johnston had earlier advertised, by "neatness, convenience, and comfort." The springs provided water; wood fires, heat; and whale-oil lamps and candles, light. "Communications between different parts of the premises," said the announcements, "are such as to cause no exposure, even in the most inclement seasons," although students were required to bring with them "thick leather shoes, sun-bonnet and shawl."

In 1853–54 a new portico set another and characteristic Hollins pattern. Virginia Daniel Woodruff, on her arrival in 1864 (East Building then in use, and Main begun) was to comment on the "long porches for promenades which are echoing from the ceaseless tramp of teachers and scholars taking the morning air." They were to do so on the West Building porches until 1900.

THE NEW PORTICO (Fig. 16) The new portico with upper balcony was built along the 140-foot frontage of the main house at a cost of $1,490. Chief woodwork designer was Gustavus Sedon, who adopted Greek Revival details from the architectural handbooks of Asher Benjamin to create these large square posts with recessed panels on their faces and straight fillets under semiclassic capitals.

Probably the "May Pole with its gorgeous, fluttering ribbons" mentioned in the *Semi-Annual* of 1898 is shown in this snapshot, made before the "old house" was torn down in 1900.

SULPHUR SPRINGHOUSE (Fig. 17) In 1854 the principal was "authorized to have a house built over the Sulphur Spring," for not more than $100. Actually when built in 1856, it cost something over $200: $150 to D. C. Yates for the house, and the rest for brickwork done by O. W. Brown and tinwork by C. Booze. Not only did it exist well into this next century (it was rebuilt in 1960), but it long provided a favorite background for countless Hollins photographers.

The therapeutic waters also remained a major attraction. Through the first ten years of the seminary, and again in the late 1850s, the academic year included the summer months "when the use of the mineral water is most beneficial." Sessions began in June and ran through March.

Nonacademic summer boarders coming to Botetourt Springs provided a source of slight income for decades. In fact, even in the twentieth century people from town continued the practice of summering on the Hollins campus, anticipating the air-conditioned institutes of the summers of the 1960s and '70s.

ENON BAPTIST CHURCH (Fig. 18) The affiliation between the seminary and Enon Church, across the highway, was, if not formal, firm and continuous. Already in 1826 one-half acre of the original property had been allotted to a "Greenridge meeting house," and now, in 1850, land was granted by the Valley Union Society to the Green Ridge Baptist Church for a new building site. Both land and structure were to revert to the Society if they should pass out of Baptist hands.

Choice of the name "Enon" was fitting, for the Biblical Enon was a place near Salim where John baptized "because water was plentiful" there. Baptisms now were held in Carvin's Creek, near the new highway bridge: in May 1870, thirteen servants in one minute. Many students were to attend Enon regularly for decades, and to profess religion there. "Nearly thirty-six" did so after a "protracted meeting" for two weeks in that same May, according to Nannie Crump Armistead's diary. And commencement exercises for the seminary, first held in the newly completed Enon on July 4, 1855, were to be repeated there for several years.

The snapshot was taken of Enon in 1914, just before the rebuilding completed in 1917.

14

III. Growth, War, and Survival

Hollins Institute, 1855–1882

FORTUNES of the seminary brightened in 1855. The first donation of $5,000, made by Mr. and Mrs. John Hollins of Lynchburg, brought many changes beyond the changing of the school's name to Hollins Institute. A new charter dedicated the property in perpetuity to education, a new board of trustees was formed, and a new seal was designed (Fig. 19). An ambitious building program was inaugurated: the long-needed new dormitory, East Building, was erected between 1856 and 1858, and another, Main, was begun in 1861. Old cottages were torn down, and a frame building containing a professor's room and a business office was put up in 1859 at the eastern end of the "big house." With physical expansion came also many other changes in the functioning of the school.

But there were difficult and often tragic years, also, and

19. Seal, 1855

times when the continued existence of Hollins Institute was very much in doubt. An epidemic of typhoid fever in 1856–57, fatal to two students, brought fear of unsanitary conditions in the old buildings and closed the school during that year. Then, after Virginia's secession in 1861, there were the long war years with their constant apprehension, insufficient income, and increasing debt. The session of 1863,

opening in May, closed early in December because of the difficulty of obtaining supplies.

Still the institute persisted; in fact, the enrollment rose to 159 in 1864. But it dropped again to 43 in the spring of 1867 as a result of another epidemic, this time of pneumonia, in which 6 students died. Immediate warfare did not touch the school, but it came close. Troops camped near Enon Church, and in 1864 General Jubal Early slept with his boots on in Mrs. Cocke's sitting room in the partially finished Main Building. Commencement at Enon in 1863 had been interrupted by the news of the Yankee burning of Salem; smoke was visible, and the Hollins coachman, George, returned from Salem with a harrowing tale of how enemy cavalry had tried to seize his horses. Eliza Horsley wrote of one night spent by girls, warmly dressed for travel, outside on the upper porch; fortunately the expected raiders did not come, for Charles Lewis Cocke was the only man left on the place.

Some student fees during these years and after were paid in provisions, some not at all. In 1867, Nannie Armistead noted in her diary that there were only two meals a day: breakfast at eight and dinner at four. That was a cold winter, too, for by March Nannie had counted forty-one snows. Students were asked to bring "bedding and table furniture" and textbooks if possible. "Amidst so much excitement, anxiety, and gloom," said Cocke to the board in 1865, "the pupils have not manifested that zest for study nor realized that degree of success which have characterized former sessions," but he added, "it is a source of gratification that we have made out so well as we have."

For the three-year period 1864–67 only a single catalogue was issued. It stated that the fall of Richmond had forced a change in the scheme of instruction. Henceforth there were to be only three departments: the normal, the collegiate, and the ornamental (music and art). The preparatory department was dropped, not to be added again until 1878, when it was felt to be necessary because some entering students were poorly prepared. The normal course, promoted by Professor Edward S. Joynes, was a pioneer development, making explicit the fact that Hollins felt obligated to prepare young women for teaching. This ran until 1878. The collegiate course offered through these years, as before, Latin, French, and English language and literature, mathematics, natural sciences, moral sciences, music, and art. A student could work for a diploma in any of these subjects. Full graduates, of whom there were only one or two a year, had to secure at least five diplomas in the academic fields, and everyone desiring a diploma had to write a terminal essay on some literary or scientific subject.

A frequently quoted statement by Cocke, made first in 1857, claimed that "the plan and policy of this school recognizes the principle that in the present state of society in our country young women require the same thorough and rigid mental training as that afforded to young men," and he began to implement it. Under its Local Notes, the *Euzelian Album* of October 1879 reported that "Hollins has been completely revolutionized and reorganized on the plan of the University of Virginia (whatever that is)." What it was, in Hollins terms, is specified in the catalogue that appeared at the close of that session. New was the offering of diplomas in what might be called area subjects—classical, scientific, and literary courses, paralleling the university's divisions. The university began stating in its catalogue of 1877 (and continuing to 1880) that "there is no *curriculum* or prescribed course of study to be pursued by every student . . . (but) thorough instruction in independent schools in all the chief branches of learning . . . allowing students to select for themselves the departments to which they are led by their special tastes and proposed pursuits in life." Degrees called proficients were offered by the university in certain single subjects (as were the Hollins diplomas), and also degrees of graduate in a school as well as bachelor of letters, bachelor of science, and bachelor of arts—these apparently imitated by the Hollins area courses. The university required that a master of arts be a graduate of six schools; Hollins from 1879 on required its full graduates to complete *six* subjects (italicized in the catalogue) rather than five, as before.

Increased requirements proved to be incentive. Although

there were still occasional years with only one full graduate, there were six for each of the first three years of the new program, and then even seven or eight. Through the first five years there were also sixteen diplomas given for the classical course, ten for the literary, and four for the scientific.

Instituted also through these years were varied academic activities. Literary societies were founded; like the Washington and Jefferson literary societies of the university, these met weekly to cultivate debate and composition and were strongly encouraged by the faculty. The Euzelian ("Zeal with Knowledge") Society of Hollins was organized in 1855, the Euepian ("Pure Diction") in 1874. Minutes of the Euzelian Society suggest that the oral readings—of *The Life of Oliver Goldsmith, The Golden Legend, The Ancient Mariner,* and selections from Edgar Allan Poe and the *Eclectic Magazine*—were not always absorbing, for too often "the spirits of loquacity were so strongly manifest" that meetings had to be adjourned. But debates were popular, as they had been earlier (James Davis had written to his mother in 1847 that his society was debating "which had the greatest effect, spirits on the drunkard or money on the miser.") The Euepians and the Euzelians debated historical matters (Was Cromwell Justified in Beheading Charles I?) or topics of general interest (Are Women Given More to Revenge than Men?). Euzelian Society members together with friends gave the nucleus for a library and reading room: three hundred books. Appeals for further donations were made in college catalogues from 1860 on. Then in 1870 the board began conferring gold medals for scholarship, for a literary or scientific essay, and for excellence in music. (Fig. 20.)

During the years after the war, Hollins Institute increasingly drew students from outside Virginia, partly because, as a sad note in the catalogue of 1876–77 explains, Virginians were impoverished, partly because more families moving south and west wanted to have their daughters experience Virginia culture. Girls came chiefly from states that had belonged to the Confederacy, but from 1873 on enrollments

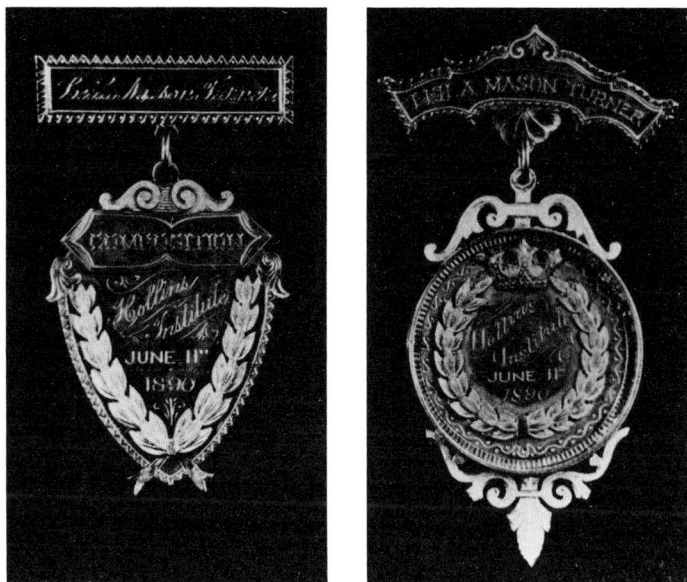

20.   Medals for scholarship

show a scattering from others; in that year, for example, two each from New York and New Jersey, one from Pennsylvania. In 1879 one appeared from Colorado. The biggest contingent came from Texas, following the arrival of the first Texan in 1868. Ten years later, there were only 47 Virginians but 28 Texans among the 118 students. The girls from Texas came by sleeping car under the conductor's care, changing only at New Orleans, from where the train brought them to Salem in a 48-hour trip. A few years later, in 1886, Hollins began to send an escort to Houston to gather up the Texas girls and others along the way. (Estes Cocke used to enjoy telling how he escorted them in his twenties, in a locked coach.)

Fund raising, however, was never successful. Charles Lewis Cocke began a capital fund drive, but it drew small response and most of the resulting pledges remained unhonored because of the war. One deeply sympathizes with his feelings after news came in 1861 of Matthew Vassar's endowing the woman's college in Poughkeepsie with $408,000. "I have never been North to ask for a cent of money," wrote Cocke, "but this school, had it been in New York State or New England, would, with its record of fifty

years clearly made public, receive all the money it needs and be adequately endowed." Nor had the northern colleges been forced to inform their patrons, as Hollins had done in the very year that Vassar opened with 353 students, that because all of the board's funds had been "lost by the sudden change of the currency of the country in 1856," planned work could not be completed.

In 1868 Cocke borrowed $10,000 for the trustees. They already owed him twice that amount, and by 1881 the institution's total indebtedness was to reach $39,000. From 1870 on the board had been offering to deed the school to Cocke, but he consistently declined. So at its meeting in 1875 the board accepted a new charter under which the fifteen trustees became corporators authorized to hold property to the value of $300,000. Colonel Tayloe was still chairman, Professor Pleasants treasurer, and Professor Turner secretary. Charles Lewis Cocke was retained as general superintendent, and, as earlier, was given commendation and free rein.

JOHN AND ANN HALSEY HOLLINS (Figs. 21, 22) John Hollins of Lynchburg gave the school its first large gift of $5,000 in 1855 and served as a member of its board until his death in 1859. It was Ann Halsey Hollins, however, who had induced her husband to support the cause of women's education, and she continued with other gifts to a total of $17,500. At a time when fees for tuition and board were $180 per year, this was a large sum. Mrs. Hollins would have given much more, said Cocke, "had her invested funds of $140,000 not all been lost by the war." The obituary on her death in 1866 commented on her "liberality without ostentation," saying that "it was contrary to her wish that her name should be associated with the institution to which she had given so generously, but she yielded to the earnest requests of the trustees."

To honor Mrs. Hollins, the board had resolved in May 1860 to "procure a portrait of herself and if possible of her deceased husband to be kept permanently in this Institute." Mrs. Hollins bequeathed to the institute these paintings, which had formerly hung in her parlor.

MILLSTONES (Figs. 23, 24) In 1954 a millstone from John Hollins's mill on Blackwater Creek, Lynchburg, was brought to be placed on front campus with other stones from old millraces at Carvin's Cove and the Trout farm on Carvin's Creek. Henry Smiley, owner of the Hollins property, donated the millstone. Standing at the left is Miss Elvira Henry Miller, great-great-granddaughter of Patrick Henry. She attended Hollins from 1867 to 1869, and in 1954, aged 103, she was Hollins's oldest living alumna.

25. East Building, 1856 lithograph

EAST BUILDING (Figs. 25–28) Construction of the elegant new East Building began in the summer of 1856, and it was ready for the 1858–59 session. The catalogue described it: "It is a three-story edifice, 144 by 36 feet, with a piazza to each floor, the entire length of the building, and contains ample Parlors and Lecture Rooms for 150 Pupils, besides a large number of private chambers." The high basement contained lecture rooms and offices, and a large flight of steps led to the main entrance above and the parlors. The structure was divided into three halls, the only communication through the upper floors being via the balconies.

With the erection of East Building the nature and orientation of the campus changed. Tinker Mountain no longer dominated; rather, an outdoor living room about two hundred by three hundred feet in size was being framed. The old cottages shown to the left in the illustration were soon to be torn down to make way for Main Building, which would make more emphatic the sense of enclosure. Activity within this space has been constant for over a century, from the early commencement festivities when local folk came to make holiday around ice cream and lemonade booths to the teach-ins and coed games of the present day.

East also reinforced the resemblance of the campus to the springs resorts, as is evident by comparing it to the lithograph of Yellow Sulphur Springs in Montgomery County, published by Ed Beyer in his *Album of Virginia*, 1855.

26. East Building, 1971

27. Old classroom in East Building

28. Beyer lithograph of Yellow Sulphur Springs, 1855

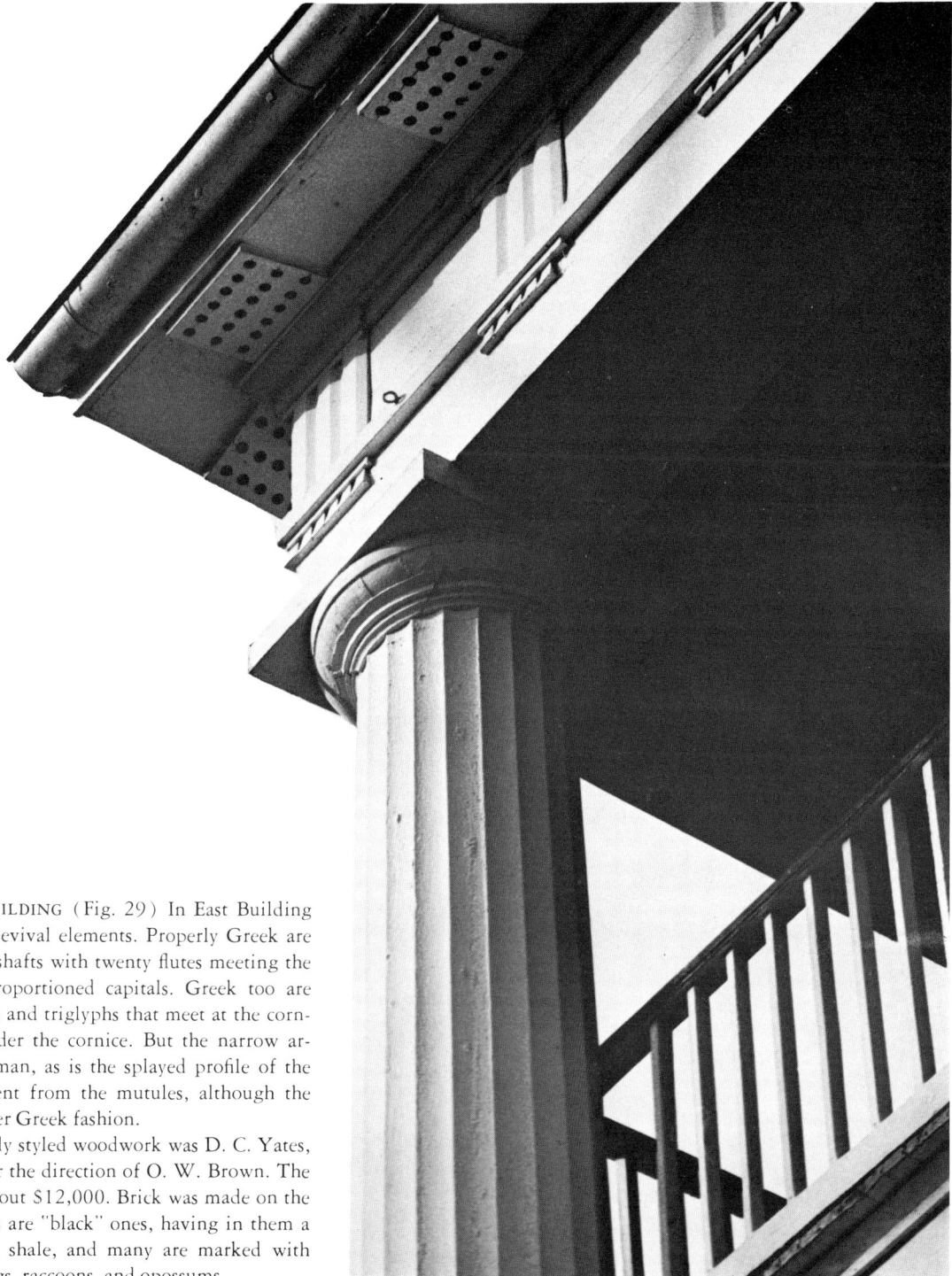

THE DORIC ORDER OF EAST BUILDING (Fig. 29) In East Building appear both Greek and Roman Revival elements. Properly Greek are the Doric columns, their tapered shafts with twenty flutes meeting the three annulets under the well-proportioned capitals. Greek too are the frieze, with its square metopes and triglyphs that meet at the corners, and the inclined mutules under the cornice. But the narrow architrave above the capitals is Roman, as is the splayed profile of the guttae. These little pegs are absent from the mutules, although the holes for them are aligned in proper Greek fashion.

The contractor for this classically styled woodwork was D. C. Yates, and the brickwork was done under the direction of O. W. Brown. The total cost for East Building was about $12,000. Brick was made on the back campus—many of the bricks are "black" ones, having in them a considerable amount of the local shale, and many are marked with footprints of chickens, turkeys, dogs, raccoons, and opossums.

PROJECTED MAIN BUILDING (Fig. 30) Main Building as envisioned would have been even more impressive than East, in fact would have been what Cocke promised the board and his patrons: "one of the most elegant edifices in the State." It was to have three floors of balconies along the entire front and ends, supported by Ionic columns (Asher Benjamin's architectural handbooks recommended the Ionic order to colleges and seminaries as being more related to arts and letters than was the Doric). The projected structure, 176 by 42 feet in plan, crowned with a cupola, would have been magnificent, but its image remains only on diplomas and catalogues of 1860.

Achieved, however, with the building of Main was the scheme of front campus: the open quadrangle favored by Thomas Jefferson, facing toward the main highway rather than toward Tinker Mountain. Within a few decades, Jeffersonian colonnades were to be added to connect the buildings.

30. Lithograph from catalogue of 1859–60

31.   Lithograph from catalogue of 1861

MAIN BUILDING (Figs. 31, 32) Contracts for Main were given in May 1860 to David Deyerle for the brickwork and to G. A. Sedon for the woodwork. The board of trustees advised the building committee—Cocke, Colonel Tayloe, T. B. Evans, and Benjamin Tinsley—"to employ an Architect to draft the building." Nowhere in the records is an architect named as such, but in August $88.59 cash was paid to Grant and Henning for a plan that was presumably for this building. It was to have a chapel and dining room, each 70 by 42 feet, and fifty-eight other chambers. Its cost, first hoped to be $10,000, was soon raised to $20,000. The committee asked early in 1861 whether the inner walls should be of wood "according to the design of the Architect" or of brick, and how the building must be heated: partitions were done in wood, and wood fires and coal grates were used until stoves replaced them in 1873.

The bricks having been made and a portion of the woodwork exe-cuted, actual building was begun on April 17, 1861. But on that day the State of Virginia seceded from the Union. Work dragged on, and brickwork and roofing were completed two years later. Sedon, unable to complete the woodwork "in the present state of the Country" had to be released from his contract, and Deyerle remained unpaid until 1882.

Sections of the building were utilized as they were completed, and after eight years even the unfinished west end of the third floor, which for so long students had called The Wilderness, was ready. Save for the back porch and cupola, Main had finally been built.

33. Central portico, Main

THE DESIGNING OF MAIN BUILDING (Figs. 33, 34) The style of Main had been much modified by necessity, but the final blend of neoclassic and Victorian was satisfying and stylish. Above an arcaded podium rose a porch with paired Ionic columns to mark the center in the pattern popularized by Charles Bulfinch and widely used since the beginning of the century, and there were projecting pavilions at the ends of the building. But Victorian brackets supported projecting cornices and baroque scrollwork filled the pediment. Instead of a formal portico, Main had a veranda with rhythmic spacing of posts, arches, and moldings.

The chapel, in which the first worship service was held on May 20, 1870, rose through two stories on the left side, and a staircase led to the porch at that end. Through the 1870s and 1880s the basement held the dining room, which was connected by a covered walkway to the old kitchen building on the site of the later dining hall.

32.   The completed Main Building

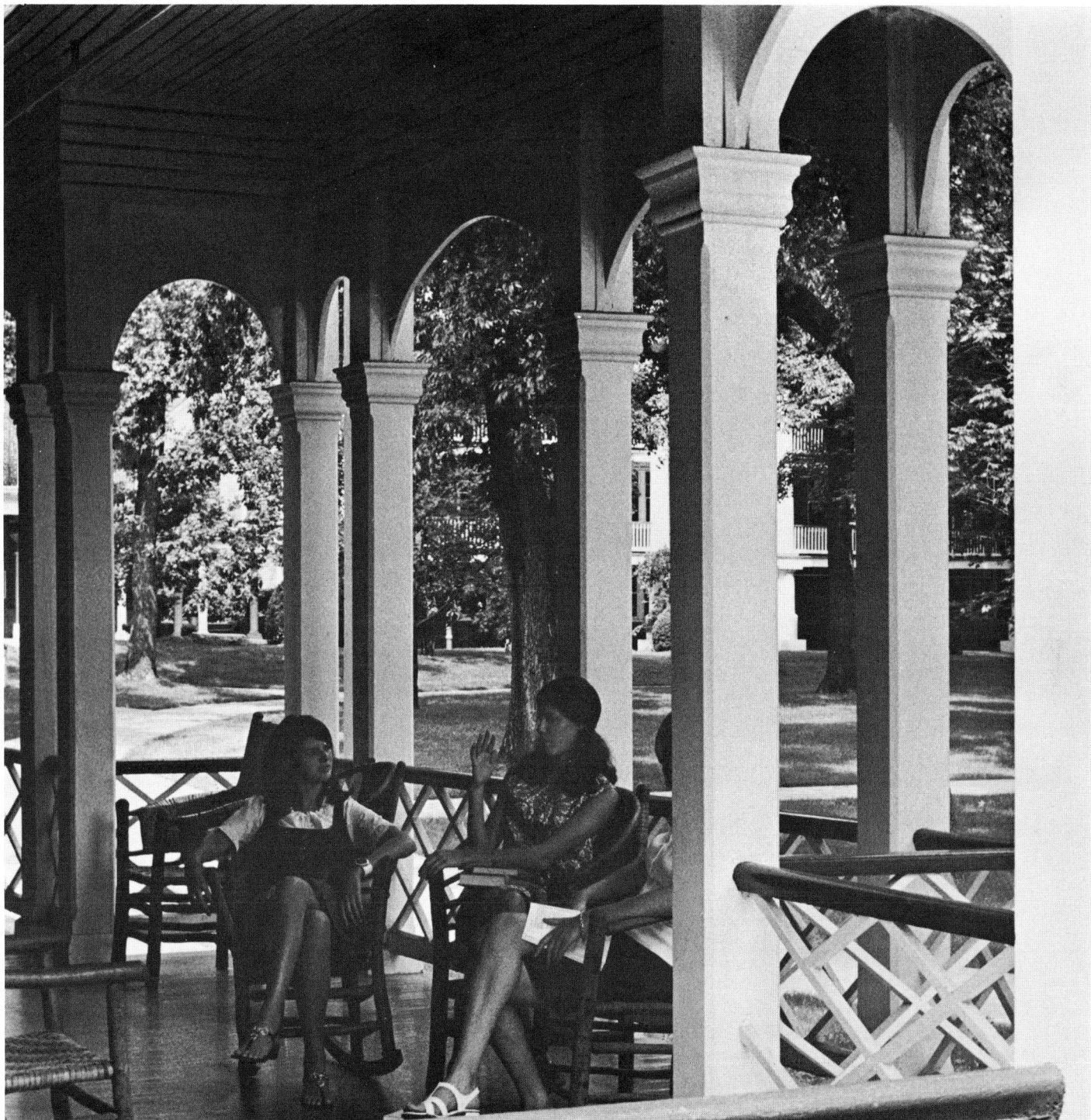

34.   Pavilion of front porch, Main

BACK CAMPUS WITH MAIN BUILDING (Figs. 35, 36) Finally in the summer of 1879 the cupola and the back porch were added to Main— "the long-promised back porch" said the *Album* reporter that June. Now the promenaders could extend their walks and the back campus had a focus to complement the sulphur spring. A relatively private roof was also available for hair drying, as a snapshot of 1907 indicates.

35. Lithograph of back campus, 1885

IV. Expansion in Late Century
The Cockes as Proprietors, 1882–1901

ON June 15, 1882, Charles Lewis Cocke, still feeling that the institution should not become a proprietary one, agreed that he and his son Charles Henry would lease the property for fifteen years at an annual rental of $3,600. The board members allowed him another $50,000 for plant improvements (they already owed him $42,000), and on that sum they were to pay the $3,000 annual interest.

Immediately Cocke gave notice of his intentions: "I shall add *twenty* additional rooms for the better accommodation of the Music and Art Departments, two large and elegant parlors, a new and capacious Chapel, a Library, and a Reading Room." The chapel was ready for the opening of the 1883–84 session. Parlor, library, and reading room were fitted into the ground floor area of the earlier chapel in Main, and new dormitory rooms were created on the second floor above these. Not only a Music and Art Hall but also a new dining room and kitchen were built by the end of the decade. By 1901 the old house, West, was completely reconstructed, so that nothing remained on the site from Botetourt Springs days save the little structure over the limestone spring.

Among further very important physical improvements, according to the principal, was creating of a new water supply. "To the variety of waters now afforded from springs and wells," he announced in the catalogue of 1885–86, "we shall add that of an elevated spring of pure freestone water on an adjacent mountain. This water is to be conveyed in pipes through the grounds and buildings, and to be used for drinking and sanitary purposes." Then in 1899 part of the property of the falls on Carvin's Creek was purchased for water power. Probably more appreciated by the students was the addition of a telephone and provision for steam heat to replace the coal fires (although the *Semi-Annual* of 1892 advises, "No more popping of corn, girls"). Beyond these there were constant minor renovations and additions, and long before the fifteen-year lease had expired much more than the $50,000 had been spent. By 1892 indebtedness of the board had grown to over $80,000, and the Cockes, too, owed thousands.

But still, as in earlier years, the institution not only continued but improved. Pictorial and literary survivals of the 1880s and 1890s have so much period charm that it is easy to forget the rigors of academic endeavor and of simple daily living. An alumna, Litsy Joynes MacFarlane, thus characterized the year 1881–82, opening this period: "a particularly hard, lean year of the many hard ones in the twenty-five years just after the war. Rooms were plainly furnished, with dressers made of three boxes nailed together; soft coal burned on open grates, and students brought their own kerosene lamps; the fare was meagre with cold bread and butter for supper, and New Orleans molasses, taken in payment of tuition for a Louisiana girl . . . every girl had a warm shawl, often her only wrap; dresses were woolen, very few girls had more than two or three, and there was probably not a silk dress of any sort on the place."

Major concerns for Charles Lewis Cocke and his staff through these late decades of the century were fostering the intellectual development of the individual young woman and preparing her for varied fields of activity. He was particularly proud of the record of Hollins alumnae in teaching and in church work, both at home and with foreign missions. Students, too, were writing and debating about the issue of women's place in society. An article in the *Euzelian Album* of 1884 remarks that "one of the warm questions of the day, and most fruitful for discussion, is this one of Woman's Rights, her sphere, her possibilities, and her future." Typical subjects for debate were Does American Society Deny to Women, as Such, Any Rights? Has the Present System of Education in America a Tendency to Unfit Women for the Home Life? and (called a "hackneyed subject" by the reporter for the *Semi-Annual* of 1890) Would Coeducation Be an Advantage to Both Sexes?

The alumna Virginia Strickler Milburne recalled her Hollins years, 1884–86, as "unbelievably serious," saying "to most of us older ones, the curriculum was the thing. And how proud we were of Hollins' high standards! We willingly worked hard for our parchments." On the other side, however, is the remark in the *Annual* of 1890: "questions concerning the wisdom of examinations and of the marking system seem to be at present agitating the faculties of colleges and schools far and wide"—a remark with a curiously modern ring. An editorial of 1890 also anticipates a scheme put into practice at Hollins in 1967, for after noting the "utterly demoralizing" effect of a two-week Christmas vacation the writer suggests that "classes should be arranged with reference to the required holiday, examinations fixed accordingly, and finished up beforehand."

The curriculum followed much the same pattern as earlier. German was added, and a program in experimental psychology was introduced in 1894 by an alumna-teacher, Miss Natalie Bowman, who had studied under Titchener at Cornell; this unfortunately was soon dropped because of her poor health. Separate diplomas, plus those for the classical, literary, and scientific courses, were still issued. To these was added in 1888 an ornamental course (French or German and music or art), and in 1889 a philosophical course (mental and moral science and history). Since no one sought the ornamental diploma, it was replaced in 1895 by the eclectic diploma. For this the student might choose any four departments, and it became understandably popular. Full graduates from 1897 on were required to complete work in eight departments.

Cocke labeled this variety "the eclectic system of instruction" and remarked that Hollins had been the first school to adopt it, soon to be followed by others. He was actually running five schools during this period: a preparatory department, a collegiate, a school of music and one of art, and one called irregular studies. This last included elocution, business practice, the Holy Bible and the Lord's Day, calisthenics, and (taught by the resident physician) anatomy, physiology, and hygiene. Soon, however, physiology was grouped with the traditional physics, chemistry, and astronomy of the science division. Calisthenics, "designed to give symmetry, elasticity, and grace to the body," was to be relabeled physical culture, then gymnastics, and finally physical training, and it flourished in the following century, being then

divorced from elocution with which it was originally paired.

Among the many influential teachers of this period several scholars stand out. There was William Taylor Thom, expert on Shakespeare, the Frenchman Théodore Louis Kusian, who taught modern languages, and Erich Rath, a German musician who was to make music a strong department and was to teach at Hollins until 1936. These, added to the Latin scholar "Uncle Billy" Pleasants, made a strong core for instruction.

Enrollments at the institute were growing, too, and more and more out-of-state candidates were accepted. In 1881–82 there were 115 students, of whom 54 were from Virginia, 21 from Texas. By 1890 there were 209: 112 Virginians, 31 Texans, 6 girls from New York, and 2 from Mexico. By 1900 there were 236 students from 24 states, including Colorado and California. And the Commissioner of Education in Washington in his report of 1890–91 had commended Hollins, saying: "An investment of a million [dollars] would place here a great school of the higher type and perpetuate the well-earned reputation of this well-known institute, for the past forty years one of the most notable of Southern schools."

Seven miles or so from Hollins Institute the town of Big Lick, incorporated in 1874, was also expanding. It received a new charter in 1884 and a new name, Roanoke. Expansion was in large measure due to its connection with the railroads, for here was the junction of the Norfolk and Western with the Shenandoah Valley. The first valley train from Hagerstown, Maryland, came into Roanoke in 1882, and soon there was a Hollins station on that line, only a little over a mile from the school.

In 1897 the lease to the Cockes was extended for another ten years. But in 1900 Charles Henry Cocke died at the age of forty-seven, and a month later Charles Lewis, still feeling strongly that private ownership of educational institutions was not desirable, agreed to accept the property in lieu of leasing it, for he had to provide for his family. The board of trustees, chaired since Colonel Tayloe's death in 1897 by

William Walter Moffett, owed Cocke by its own estimate over $101,000. A new charter was now issued by the General Assembly of Virginia, dated February 2, 1901, and a new Board of Governors appointed, all save Professor Kusian, members of the Cocke family.

On May 4, 1901, Charles Lewis Cocke died, having devoted to Hollins Institute fifty-five of his eighty-one years. Susanna Pleasants Cocke died five years later. Both were buried in the family graveyard on the hill overlooking the group of handsome brick buildings that now filled the hollow beside the sulphur spring.

37. The chapel, 1883

BRADLEY CHAPEL (Figs. 37–39) The new chapel, named in the 1930s for Joshua Bradley, was erected in 1883. In style it still retained some classic elements: Roman blind arcades and Tuscan capitals, and it harmonized with East and Main. A long list of supplies purchased and workers paid appears in the ledger for 1883; chief builders appear to have been G. A. Sedon and George W. Etter. Bricks— 150,000—were made and burned on the site of the later president's house.

By its placement the chapel tightened further the effect of enclosure of the campus. Early lithographs show the boarded "covered way" that ran between the buildings, so that students could have no excuse for avoiding classes or chapel services in inclement weather.

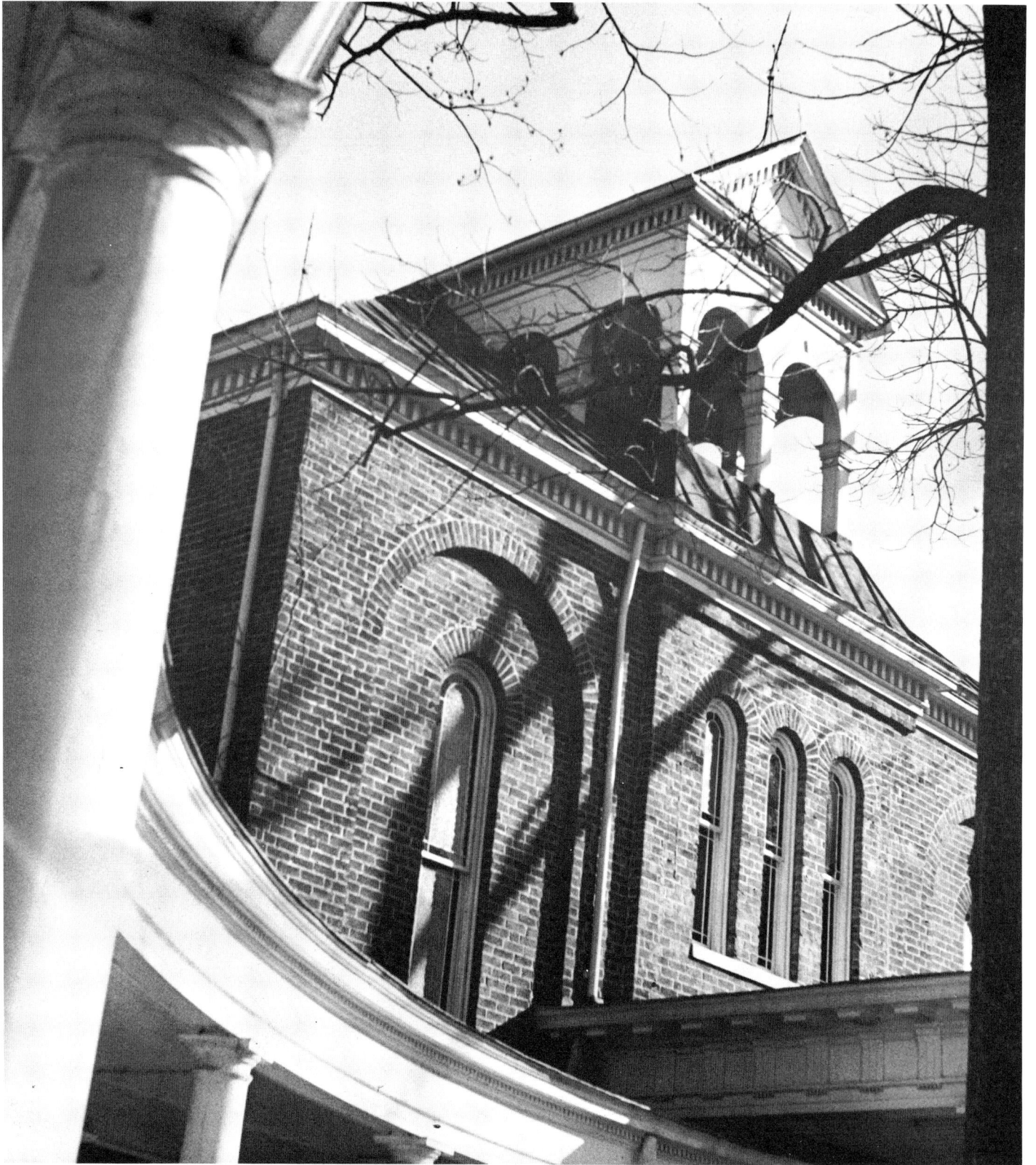

38. Detail of exterior, Bradley Chapel, 1946

39. Columns of Bradley and East

40. Interior of chapel after 1915

INTERIOR, BRADLEY CHAPEL (Fig. 40) In addition to the audience room seen here, the chapel had ten music rooms on the ground floor. It was kept heated day and night, because pupils came for private devotions in the early morning hours and school worship services were held daily after supper. In the 1880s, Hollins had four regular chaplains: Presbyterian, Lutheran, Baptist, and Episcopalian, with an occasional Methodist preacher.

From 1852 on, the seminary had had a melodeon, which in 1882 was given to G. A. Sedon in lieu of $10 cash payment for his carpentry work. A new two-manual, two-octave organ was installed in Bradley in 1883 and used until 1915, when it was replaced by a three-manual Moeller organ. To accommodate this, the chapel was extended to its present length of seventy feet. For practicing, there was also a reed organ used from 1870 until 1892 when a new one was purchased.

41. Music and Art Hall, 1889 lithograph

MUSIC AND ART HALL (Figs. 41–43) Studio art, like music, attracted many students whose work was already being exhibited annually in the calisthenics hall of East Building. Now they had two "large airy studios with well-tinted walls and fine skylights" in a new building, erected at a cost of $5,127.33 while H. L. Pauli was director of music. Two stories in height, the brick building rose impressively behind the chapel, on the site where William Carvin's fortified house had stood. Across the front ran Victorian double-storied balconies ("the indispensable portico" remarked the *Semi-Annual* reporter; now "more than 1000 feet of piazza" advertised Cocke), with a large staircase up to the main entrance. There were side entrances, too, and a covered passageway connecting the hall with Main Building. High narrow arched windows and trim reflected late-nineteenth-century taste. In addition to the studios, the building held varied offices and practice rooms.

Its interior was completely remodeled when it was converted to faculty apartments in 1926 and renamed Carvin House. The porches were removed, and a new doorway copied from that of Westover, the Byrd homestead on the James River, added a Georgian touch with its heavy scrolls flanking a pineapple, traditional symbol of hospitality.

44.   Music Ensemble, 1888

MUSICAL ENSEMBLES (Figs. 44, 45) Music was always a favored subject at Hollins Institute. Although, in Professor Erich Rath's judgment,
it had been a "parlor accomplishment," it was now academically viable,
for it could be offered as one of the areas required for the full diploma.
The Music Ensemble with Miss Thalia Hayward was photographed in
1888, the orchestra with director Louis Alberti in 1900.

45. Orchestra, 1900

CHARLES HENRY COCKE AND STUDENTS (Fig. 46) Under the terms of the new contract of 1882, Charles Henry Cocke shared with his father the lease of the property and served as business manager of Hollins Institute until his death in 1900. Charles Lewis, lamenting his son's early death, said he was "the most efficient, successful and progressive officer Hollins ever had." Dorothy Vickery reported in her 1942 history of Hollins that "everybody loved Mr. Charlie . . . he was a cheerful companion in any company and was accessible at all times to both students and faculty." Shown to the right of Mr. Charlie in this photograph taken in 1886 is Miss Belle Lester, superintendent of the dining room.

PROFESSOR PLEASANTS AND LATIN CLASS (Fig. 47) "Uncle Billy" Pleasants, Mrs. Cocke's brother, was a key figure at Hollins from his arrival in 1852 until his death in 1914. Except for a short time spent teaching at Bellevue Academy, he devoted his energies to Hollins. He was a Latin scholar who at times also taught natural science and philosophy, in later years became dean of the faculty, and was given an honorary degree of Doctor of Laws by Washington and Lee University. Student comments describe him as colorful and often caustic, but as regarded with respect and remembered with affection.

PROFESSOR THOM WITH FULL GRADUATES OF 1886 (Fig. 48) William Taylor Thom, at Hollins from 1879 to 1889, inaugurated here the study of Shakespeare, which was notably progressive; at Yale, for example, courses in Shakespeare began in 1875. In the 1880s the New Shakespeare Society of England gave annual prizes for the best examination papers on the plays, and Hollins winners brought its first international fame to the institute. In 1881 Hannah Wilson and Emma Mertins won awards for their *Hamlet* examinations, and in 1882 Natalie Bowman for her *Macbeth* paper. In 1882, also, a Shakespeare Reading Club was organized at Hollins, and Professor Thom, in response to questions about his teaching methods, wrote his *Shakespeare and Chaucer Examinations,* which was published in 1883.

PROFESSOR A. T. L. KUSIAN (Fig. 49) Professor Kusian, foreign agent during the war for the Confederate government, sought an interview with Charles Lewis Cocke after hearing him speak at a meeting in Danville in 1889. He came to Hollins to teach and remained for thirty years until his death in 1920. In addition to being professor of modern languages, Kusian served for nineteen years as secretary and for five as dean of the faculty.

Professor Kusian taught French and German, but, wrote Marguerite Hearsey for the *Spinster* in 1921, "from astronomy to medicine, from Plato's *Republic* to Darwin's *Origin of the Species,* the class would be led in one short hour" in a discourse peppered with sarcasm for superficial literary critics and by the "sir!" with which he addressed his pupils. Dr. Kusian was "eccentric, lovable, inspiring" to generations of students. He was also the only nonfamily member of the Board of Governors of the institute.

38

DINING HALL (Fig. 50) The choice of an octagonal plan for the "new dining hall with culinary attachments" was fitting in the intimate scheme of the campus. The octagon, favored for domestic building in the South, neatly filled a corner of the quadrangle and echoed the polygonal shape of the springhouse. On the ground floor of the brick structure were apartments and offices. A Victorian gallery above faced both front and back campus and provided an airy note with its little ornamental drops centered between bracketed posts. Arched doors and windows opened into a domed hall, sixty feet in diameter; the angles of its octagonal base were marked by even more exuberantly carved brackets.

The building, named Botetourt Hall in the early 1930s, was completed in time for Thanksgiving dinner in 1890. Its total cost was $7,732. A ledger entry of July 8, 1890, reads, "To cash, Architect: $160.00," but unfortunately he remains anonymous, although other names are multiple. C. Nininger received $1,000 for brick, G. A. Sedon was foreman, G. W. Etter was a major carpenter, and about $800 was paid to McGcc and Ragan for cash and board to "hands." Paint came from Evans and Chalmers and from O. D. Oakey, and blinds, ceiling, and brackets were supplied by Adams and Woodson.

51. Christmas dinner decorations

52. Lithograph of back campus, 1890

CHRISTMAS DINNER (Fig. 51) A long-continued tradition was that of decorating the Christmas tables with tiny trees bearing lighted candles, and of making the occasion festive with carols sung by students, faculty, and servants.

BACK CAMPUS (Fig. 52) Although the new buildings did not as yet extend into back campus, this area was developing a personality of its own, as this lithograph from the catalogue of 1890–91 suggests. The sulphur spring was still frequently visited, and its waters found to be externally beneficial. ("We are bleaching for Commencement early this year. How fair we will be, to be sure!" wrote a Hollins girl in 1878.)

SERVANTS (Fig. 53) Between the campus and Tinker Mountain there grew up a community where servants lived, many in log cabins. One of the longest in service was Caesar Morton, at Hollins from 1865 to 1929. Caesar said he had worked here "ever since de fus year Gen'l Lee surrendered," and boasted of having shaken hands with William Jennings Bryan, whose daughter Grace was a student. Waiting on table in buttermilk time, Caesar would say to the girls, "Lait or l'eau or lactum?"

A familiar sight for a long time was that of the women bringing back fresh laundry. The 1903 *Spinster* related that there were "sometimes four or five in line, balancing on their heads huge baskets, filled to overflowing with snowy garments, a piece of gaudy calico or pink mosquito net spread over the top."

WEST, JOHNSTON & CO. RICHMOND VA.

54. Lithograph of front campus, 1891

55. Right wing of West Building

NEW WINGS, WEST BUILDING (Figs. 54, 55) By 1890 the "old house" was in poor condition and a total rebuilding was necessary, but financial pressures forced the change to come in stages. First erected were three-story brick wings, giving about thirty new rooms at a cost of $13,240.18. C. Nininger supplied brick, G. R. Ragan supervised its laying; G. A. Sedon, George Etter, and H. M. Bower did the woodwork. In style these wings were like the new Music and Art Hall, spare and high-ceilinged with long narrow windows, and with double Victorian galleries facing the dining hall. The left wing held infirmary, doctor's office, and faculty living quarters, and the right wing's upper story had two large halls for the Euzelian and Euepian societies.

EUZELIAN OFFICERS (Fig. 57) For their meetings Euzelian members wore the Oxford cap and gown. In the 1880s they were reading works of Longfellow, Milton, Tennyson, Whittier, Byron, Shelley, and Mrs. Browning.

56. Euzelian Hall, 1895

EUZELIAN HALL (Fig. 56) The Euzelians, disbanded in 1862, reorganized in 1873 and began in 1878 to publish *The Album*, a monthly magazine with news, essays, and creative writing. At last in 1893, instead of the uncomfortable old rooms lighted first by tallow candles and then by oil lamps (for which in 1858 "five virgins were appointed to trim the lamps and to procure oil and have it ready"), the Euzelians had a grand new hall and sixty-four members. Presents given for the opening included a bust of Homer and a "beautiful piano lamp." A little later, alumnae from Oregon sent a Japanese vase, and then a white fur rug was acquired to adorn the president's stand. The tapestry-canvas, based on Alma-Tadema's *A Reading from Homer*, was made by society members aided by the art teacher, Miss Newton.

57. Euzelian officers, 1900

EUEPIAN HALL (Fig. 58) The Euepian Literary Society's special production was the annual celebration of Robert E. Lee's birthday. But members collaborated with the Euzelians in publishing first *The Annual* and then a *Semi-Annual,* issued regularly from 1888 on. In 1897–98 this was combined with the *Spinster,* which alone has lasted to the present day.

Euepians met each Saturday night in their new hall, which was perhaps more colorful than the Euzelian one, for within a few years it had a "handsome metallic ceiling" and "crimson hangings about the rostrum, the mirror, and the windows." A custom-made mirror was purchased from a Philadelphia firm in 1895 for $145; it was almost ten feet high, with an elaborately gilded frame and a marble-topped shelf at its base. (This mirror, hung for a long time in Main drawing room, is now back in West, in one of the parlors.) Among other furnishings donated for the new hall were copies of Guido Reni's *Aurora* and of a portrait of Charlotte Corday.

NEW CENTER, WEST BUILDING (Fig. 59) The board had specified at its meeting in 1890 that West Building be redone "with a handsome portico." This was finally accomplished with the complete rebuilding of the central portion in 1900 by Lewton and Kirkbride, contractors from Roanoke. Their contract was for $5,000, but costs ran some $400 higher. The portico echoed that of Main Building: paired columns ran above an arcaded podium (the red brickwork of this was painted white in 1959). Surmounting the gabled attic with its Palladian window was a delicate cupola borne on a ring of columns like a classic tholos, and from this rose a tall flagstaff.

On the ground floor were parlors, apartments, and a "cozy" room for the YWCA, which had been organized in 1888. A typical student room above these, described in the *Semi-Annual* of 1901, was pleasingly furnished with "highly polished oak furniture, bright heavy drugget, white enamelled bedstead, student's table and bookshelves." Through the succeeding decade the students rooming in West were listed as being in "the Waldorf"—a neat contrast to East, which had become the "Tinnyment."

MRS. ELIZA SPEIDEN CHILDS (Fig. 61) Mrs. Childs, who for twenty-four years was Lady Principal at Hollins Institute, gave an aristocratic tone to social life there. As daughter of Commodore William Speiden, explorer of the South Seas, she was a native of Washington, D.C., and grew up in a society distinguished by administrative, diplomatic, and army and navy people and customs. Widowed, Mrs. Childs came to Hollins with her two children in 1873, and stayed to work closely under Charles Lewis Cocke as the first of the "social deans."

SENIOR PARLOR (Fig. 60) The senior parlor on the third floor of West, shown with a popular "Turkish corner" in this photograph of 1902, was shifted in 1904 to East "Tinnyment." But a sketch in the 1907 *Spinster* indicates that the same furnishings were retained, and presumably the same mood expressed. A jingle accompanies the sketch:

> The cool Cositorium is where you may rest,
> Or talk with your darling, if that you like best.
> Sweet strains of music will while away care,
> And a brush is provided to smooth up the hair.

"Darlings" were close girl friends; no boys were admitted.

SOCIAL ACTIVITIES (Figs. 62–67) Social regulations were strict: girls might, for example, go to Roanoke to shop on Saturday but were never permitted to attend evening affairs there. Naturally there was a good bit of home-planned entertainment, and social clubs were beginning to multiply. Often the Cotillion Club gave a german, and its members, as the *Semi-Annual* reporter remarked, "were the gentlemen pro tem. of the occasion, and a more gallant set it would be hard to find." The Kentucky Club of 1899, reported the same magazine, was "probably the largest and most regular in all its social functions and gatherings."

There was, as always before, constant promenading, particularly over the bridge that spanned the shallow ground at the open side of the quadrangle. There were walks and picnics along the creek, to the falls, to the mountains, and usually in the spring a two-day trip to the Natural Bridge. Literary societies produced plays, and students and faculty put on varied entertainments such as minstrel shows. May Day, too, was celebrated.

63. Kentucky Club page in *Spinster,* 1900

64. The old bridge

65. Carvin's Creek

66. Mandolin and Guitar Club, 1900

67. *The School for Scandal,* 1901

68. Climbing Tinker, ca. 1898

TINKER DAY (Figs. 68, 69) " 'Off to the mountains! No school to-day!' 'Is it true? Did Mr. Cocke say that?' 'Well, there go the men carrying the lunch.' Soon the bell rings, and the girls assemble, some with baskets and long sticks, some with bright faces, for Tinker Day is one of the red-letter days in the Hollins calendar. Then, 'all is ready!' and away they go."

Thus reads the article on Tinker Day in the *Semi-Annual* of February 1897. There were actually two Tinker Days in the 1880s, one in the fall and one in the spring, on Saturdays. But it did not become an official holiday until 1895 and was then set for a designated day in October. In 1899 the surprise element that continues was introduced, with the exact time a secret, as Mrs. Cocke remarked, between "Charles and the Lord." After the turn of the century, it appeared on the college calendar for coming sessions, being recognized as equal to Christmas and Easter.

69. Riding to Tinker, 1901

70.   Sports page in *Spinster,* 1900

71.   Basketball team, 1898–99

SPORTS (Figs. 70–72) Rival basketball teams—Red (for awhile Green and White) and Blue (or Blue and Black)—were set up in 1897. Long before that Hollins girls had been active; they had always walked, for one thing. The catalogue of 1889–90 stated that "girls at boarding schools must take much physical exercise . . . failing to do this, they wilt and wither and make feeble women." It also put into italics the information that "all young ladies attending this Institute must be provided with thick walking-shoes, rubber overshoes, warm cloaks or shawls, and woolen hoods. They must also have warm clothing, especially underwear. We live in a bracing climate and spend much time in the open air."

Croquet had been introduced in the 1870s, and in the 1880s and 1890s girls were forming tennis clubs and were bicycling, tobogganing, and ice skating. But team sports came in only at the very end of the century, and the first of these was basketball, adopted in 1896, very soon after it had been introduced as an activity for women. It was learned at Hollins from a rule book. The *Roanoke Times* reported of an early game that during the first half each team made one basket, but in the second half, since neither side "succeeded in entangling the sphere in the net so temptingly suspended above them, the game was called when darkness intervened."

72.   Tobogganing, ca. 1900

73. Mohican Team of 1902

TEAMS (Fig. 73) Permanent basketball teams were organized in 1900 and given Indian names and totems. Mohicans wore blue sweaters bearing their golden turtle totem, and Yemassees wore red, with the device of an arrow piercing a black letter *Y*. The final match was played on Thanksgiving Day and was followed by a banquet, setting up a tradition that continued well into the twentieth century. But not for fifty years has there been such festooning of gates, dormitories, and bleachers as there was in the early decades.

FACULTY AND STAFF, CA. 1895 (Fig. 74) Included in the group in
front of the ornamental fountain and gas lamps flanking the Main
Building steps are *front row, left to right:* Mrs. Leila Turner (English), W. O. Whitescarver (mathematics), Miss R. B. Hurt (Latin
assistant), William H. Pleasants (Latin), Mrs. Charles L. Cocke,
Charles L. Cocke, Eliza S. Childs, A. T. L. Kusian (modern languages), Mary W. Jackson (dramatics), Mrs. E. A. Crutchfield (ma-
tron); *back row:* Charles H. Barnwell (English), Louise D. Hardesty
(mathematics), Belle Lester (housekeeper), Marion S. Bayne (librarian), Genevieve Rudd (preparatory school teacher), Matty L.
Cocke (registrar), Dr. Richard T. Style (physician), Virginia D.
Cole (nurse), Thalia Hayward (music), Mrs. S. K. Knight (voice),
Mary Pleasants (music), Charles Henry Cocke (business manager),
Erich Rath (music), Kate Weaver (violin).

75. Charles Lewis Cocke in buggy, 1880s

GOLDEN WEDDING ANNIVERSARY AND JUBILEE (Figs. 75–77) When the Cockes celebrated their golden wedding anniversary on the last day of 1890, they were presented with a full-length portrait painted by a daughter-in-law, Lelia Maria Smith Cocke, and commissioned by six hundred alumnae, all of whom sent cards to be put into a commemorative album. The portrait, showing Cocke presenting a diploma, was hung in the parlor, "beautifully draped in dark red and raised from the floor on a platform covered with red," according to the *Semi-Annual*. A fine study of Mrs. Cocke was painted by Lelia Cocke in 1895.

There was to come also a golden jubilee, celebrating Charles Lewis Cocke's fiftieth year at Hollins. This was held on June 2, 1896, and attended by some sixty alumnae, who remained to form an Alumnae Association. Plans made and dues set at twenty-five cents, the alumnae disbanded to meet again in June 1897 to act on the constitution and bylaws. The first alumnae banquet was held in 1897 in the dining hall, at 10 P.M.; present were sixty alumnae. "Many and unique were the toasts and the responses," reported the *Semi-Annual*, "all drunk in sulphur water fresh and cool from the dear old spring."

76. The Cockes in their sitting room in Main

77.   Portrait of Susanna Cocke, 1895

78.   President Matty L. Cocke

V. From Institute to College

Miss Matty Cocke's Presidency, 1901–1933

WHEN Miss Matty Cocke at age forty-five became the first woman president of any college in Virginia, her only academic qualification was her full diploma from Hollins Institute. But through a quarter-century she had taught mathematics, acted as librarian and registrar and as secretary to her father, and become thoroughly conversant with the workings of the institution.

On May 5, 1901, she sent out the official announcement of Cocke's death and named the people whom he had designated to succeed him. Beside herself as president—a new title, for Charles Lewis had been called principal or superintendent—Lucian H. Cocke, her brother, was vice-president, and Frank W. Duke, newly married to her niece, was secretary-treasurer. One nephew, Joseph A. Turner, became business manager and the other, M. Estes Cocke, superintendent of buildings and grounds. The Board of Governors included these five plus professors William E. Pleasants and A. T. L. Kusian.

On the staff inherited by Miss Matty were several people who were to stay with her through her tenure: M. Estes Cocke in physics and chemistry, Agnes C. Terrell in history and political economy, Thalia Hayward in music and botany, Marian S. Bayne as registrar and librarian, and Willie M. Scott as secretary to the president. Others who would remain a decade or more were "Uncle Billy" Pleasants in classics, Professor Kusian in modern languages, Mary Pleasants in music, history, and Latin, Lucie P. Stone in art, G. W. Drake as resident physician and teacher of physiology, and Maria F. Parkinson, lady principal.

Erich and Leila Rath, after a short time away, returned in 1907 to teach music and German. They remained through Miss Matty's presidency as did others appointed in that first decade: George Braxton Taylor as first resident chaplain and teacher of Bible, Bessie Cocke Barbee and Elizabeth Kellam as supervisors of the dormitories and the infirmary, Charles N. Dickinson to teach mathematics and Greek, Miss Mary Williamson to teach first English and then philosophy, Bettie G. Dickinson to serve as secretary and cashier, and Bessie K. Peyton assisting variously with

English, the choir, and recording. Arriving with this group, again to stay ten years or more, were F. A. Cummings, Loulie A. Snead, and Alma Boyd in English, and Carl Hoffman in music.

Through the first several years, announcement of each change was accompanied by the comment that it was what Charles Lewis Cocke had planned: for example, the power plant, the sewerage system, the new and larger reservoir on the mountain. And Miss Matty (the form of address she preferred) maintained the close family atmosphere that Hollins had enjoyed, in her intimate concern for and relationship with students, staff, and alumnae.

But the younger generation took over, and changes multiplied. Her energetic nephews were progressive and the students rapidly developed more initiative and assumed more responsibility. Then, too, where Charles Lewis Cocke had built a school and its curriculum in an open field, as it were, Miss Matty's concern had to be the meeting of standards set by other colleges and accrediting agencies in a competitive period. Conservative progress was not enough for the reputation of the school or indeed for its survival. So under Miss Matty, whose nature was not aggressive nor scholarly, who attended few outside meetings, wrote few articles, undertook no active fund-raising, the college advanced. Had she been more forceful there would have been less chance for student initiative, for example; the girls would have loved Miss Matty less and themselves accomplished less. Miss Matty seems to have served the role of catalyst engendering a spirit of mutual cooperation among administration, faculty, students, and alumnae, delegating authority to those who were eager and able to assume it, and achieving, by the close of her term, a college plant of considerable value and an academic program of recognized worth.

In retrospect then—and to many of her contemporaries—it seems that Miss Matty was ideal as president for this transitional period. By its close, more buildings had been erected than ever before, a system of student government was well established, and the school had returned from family management to the control of a board of trustees, under the requisite endowment raised in a commendable alumnae campaign. Again the school was hit by a major war, but happily with none of the earlier grief of Reconstruction. True, there was never enough money, but that was a normal condition for Hollins.

The catalogue of 1901–2 announced the first academic change, to a four-year program leading to the degree of bachelor of arts. At first this did not seem to be too different from the former full graduate diploma, for A.B. candidates were to complete work in eight departments (English language, English literature, Latin, French or German, history, mathematics, physics or chemistry or botany, and moral science), and it was still possible to graduate in a single department or course. There were still no entrance requirements, and an academic certificate, or A.C., could be obtained for two years' work or for four diplomas. In 1903 three girls received the A.B., and in the courses nine achieved the eclectic, four the classical, and two each the literary and philosophical degrees.

But with the session of 1904–5, a decisive change was evident in the rigid four-year program then established. Through the first two years, English and composition, Latin or Greek, French or German, history, and mathematics were required. The third year added to required courses chemistry or physics, and biology or mathematics, and offered one elective: history of art or music theory. The fourth year allowed choice of four subjects chosen from those mentioned, or astronomy or political economy, but also required the culminating literary or scientific essay formerly expected of full graduates.

Then in 1909 came the announcement that the A.C. was to be discarded and that specific admission requirements, the fourteen Carnegie units, had to be met. The still rigid four-year program remained, save that the applicant, if already skilled in Latin, could take history rather than an ancient language in her freshman year. Now all students also had to take Bible courses, and in 1910 they went on a six-day weekly schedule; no longer was Monday a free day. "O

Tempora! O Mores!" lamented a reporter for the *Quarterly* that November, "forever in the annals of Hollins life will this year 1909–10 be a memorable one. . . . Henceforth, Hollins with its comfortable special courses is no more; we have become a more exact college. . . . Our curriculum has at last succumbed."

Henceforth, indeed, the institute was no more. In 1910 its name was changed to Hollins College, and in 1911 to Hollins College, Incorporated, with a new charter granted by the General Assembly.

Hollins had fallen in line with other institutions, and from 1913 on its A.B.s were admitted to full graduate standing at institutions such as Columbia University—the school's reputation backed of course by the fact that earlier alumnae had done marvelously well in graduate schools such as those of Radcliffe and the University of Chicago. Through the years before World War I there were from ten to twelve A.B. degrees given annually, the eighteen of 1910 being exceptional, in a total enrollment averaging about 250. When enrollments increased to about 340 through the 1920s and early 1930s, the average number of A.B.s conferred was about thirty-eight, with highs of fifty-four to fifty-six in 1927, 1931, and 1932.

The curriculum remained structured, but allowed for some variation. Majors in two related subjects were introduced in 1915–16, and the following session students were selecting major groups from the only three available: languages, science, or history and philosophy. The practice of naming graduates in single departments was finally discontinued in 1917, and in 1918–19 the preparatory and irregular departments were dropped. Also after the war began the scheme that was to persist for several decades: students in the upper classes chose one major subject and a related minor. Majors were then available in biology, chemistry, English, French, Latin, history, mathematics, and philosophy. Some new departments were added: zoology in 1919, economics and sociology in 1922. Applicants in the late 1920s had to offer fifteen Carnegie units, at least three of them in French or Latin, and from 1929 on had to rank at least in the upper half of their preparatory classes. The right of the better students to work independently was finally recognized in 1928 with the initiation of an honors group for girls with high averages, who might cut classes at their discretion.

Meanwhile, a school of music directed by Erich Rath was running concurrently with the college. A bachelor of music degree, first conferred in 1921, was offered until 1933. Candidates for this B.M. degree, announced in the 1918–19 catalogue, had to have the regular academic units for admission and had to take prescribed courses in English, a modern language, history of art, psychology, and (like everyone else) physical education through the first two years. The number of B.M. degrees ranged from one or two in the early years to eight in 1924 and 1929. A first six-week summer course in music was given in 1924.

Replacements and additions through these years recruited an equally loyal group of faculty and staff members who were to remain to serve Hollins after Miss Matty had retired, some through two or more succeeding presidents. Appointed between 1910 and 1920 were Adelaide Campbell in music, alumnae Rachel Wilson in French and Margaret Scott in history, and F. Lamar Janney in English. Mrs. Carrie Boozer came to act as dietitian from 1912 on.

Then in the early 1920s came Ida Sitler, Harriett Fillinger, and Goldena Farnsworth to teach biology, chemistry, and physics, and E. Marion Smith for classics. From 1925 arrived Laura Gustafson for French and Latin, Susie Blair for drama, Grace Chevraux for physical education and Major C. O. Graves as riding instructor, and Charlotte Tiplady as librarian. Eunice Barry Wigmore came to work in the business office and Mary Louise Maddrey to be in charge of student life and social affairs. Also appointed during this time were Gladys Palmer in economics and sociology, Marguerite Hearsey in English, John McGinnis in psychology, and Fanona Knox as registrar; all were to stay a number of years. And among Miss Matty's last appointees in the early 1930s were Mary Parmenter in English, Donald Bolger in music, Mary Phlegar Smith in economics and sociology, and Mrs. Elizabeth Poulton to work with Miss Maddrey.

There were in fact relatively few short-term faculty or staff members; rather, there was notable continuity and solidarity.

Perhaps the faculty members played no greater part in running the college than they had played in the nineteenth century, but a more formal participation is suggested by the listings of faculty committees. These appeared in 1910–11, with eight committees of three members each, dealing variously with academic matters (classification, special exams, library), with extracurricular affairs (lectures and concerts, Founder's Day), and with student activities (athletics, publications). There was also an advisory committee. These continued to increase in number and in personnel. A committee for freshman advising (seven women) was created in 1922, and in 1924 came the first deanship, held by Miss Mary Williamson. Orientation of freshmen began in the following year.

But the students, despite the structured program and the advising, were organizing for themselves. The change to the A.B. degree brought with it, according to the *Quarterly* of December 1902, a new spirit, one of "class-fellowship," previously experienced only by graduating classes. Now came discussion, too, of the values of a general Student Organization: of a body in which the student "must vote, serve on a committee, or perhaps, hold an office," suggested as good for developing executive ability and preparing for community service. But the reporter of this remarked, "We do not know whether or not we are yet ready to adopt this suggestion." It took time, but by the late 1920s students had assumed judicial, executive, and legislative powers.

The physical structure of the college was greatly augmented in some twenty years, to remain practically unchanged until the 1950s. Before World War I were erected a library, infirmary, science building, four faculty homes, and a complete farm with new barns and stables. After the war came the Little Theatre, a gymnasium, a new music building, a duplex apartment, and a president's house. Facilities were all improved during this period. Parts of old buildings, like the hall of Main, were extensively renovated. By 1928 the Roanoke firm of Frye and Stone was working on a comprehensive plan for further expansion. To the central quadrangle there were now extensions and some subsidiary quadrangles, plus an established faculty row in East Court.

The social life of the students seems today, like their curricula, limited and structured. Gentlemen might call in 1925, for example, only on weekend nights and Sunday afternoons. Dates for dances off campus required not only chaperones but parental permission. The 1925 *Spinster,* however, states that "two years of rapid change" had given the students the privilege of skipping meals, and that juniors and seniors were now permitted to chaperone freshmen on the buses to Roanoke. Other buses and taxis took students to Roanoke for train departures. For the Christmas rush in 1926 (by that year there were thirty-two passenger trains daily through Roanoke) the Norfolk and Western hired twenty extra porters, and the Traveler's Aid stood ready to gather up lost articles. According to the newspaper account, "everybody must be kissed and demonstrations of grief will in most cases be in order. The job of bustling onto trains 400 girls, each bent on saying goodbye to 399 others and each equipped with enough baggage for about three men will occupy the time of the station persons, however, and so they will be unable to enjoy the situation."

In 1920 faculty consent had been needed to let Clifford Devereux and his players present Ibsen's *Ghosts;* permission was forthcoming because the faculty had decided that the girls "will learn to realize that social problems do exist." But social life certainly seems unlimited when one begins to enumerate the plays and stunts and pageants, the teas and picnics, the cotillions and fashion shows, or to read of the delight in the coming of movies to Bradley Chapel in 1920 (John Barrymore in *Here Comes the Bride,* Mary Miles Minter in *Anne of Green Gables,* Mae March in *The Cinderella Man*).

In contrast to these diversions, however, came the war work, the many serious essays in the journals, the first mock election of 1920 (Harding versus Coolidge), the growing social consciousness of the 1920s. Hollins, for example, was one of the very few southern colleges cooperating in the National Student Forum, labeled by the *Manufacturer's Record* a "Trend to Socialism and Other Evils," but described by President McCracken of Vassar as arising from the "desire of American students to hear a presentation of different theories of the State and social organization," and seen by others as in part "a rebellion of youth against war." The Hollins experience was still, through Miss Matty's regime, a time of home-centered entertainment, of sentiment and of support of tradition, and of a good bit of gaiety, but it was also a time of sobriety and increasing sophistication.

But until Hollins should become divorced from proprietary ownership and revert to public control, the college could not obtain the recognition and accreditation it had to have. Altruistically, the Board of Governors offered in 1924 to relinquish control of the property, then appraised at $1.25 million, in return for a cash settlement, later fixed at $50,000 ($5,000 annually for ten years) plus annuities not to exceed $9,000 per year for a limited number of older members of the family.

This offer was publicized in May 1925, and at commencement the alumnae were asked if they would take charge of working out the details and raising the endowment. Here again they proved their loyalty in their enthusiastic acceptance. A charter was granted on December 30, 1926, to a new board of trustees, which met the following January 28 to plan for the transfer and the raising of funds. By agreement the board included three Hollins alumnae: Bessie C. Randolph, Marguerite Hearsey, and Virginia Lee Cox. Officers were D. D. Hull, Jr., president, W. C. Stephenson, vice-president, Charles I. Lunsford, treasurer, all from Roanoke, and Joseph A. Turner, secretary and business manager. Other local trustees were C. Edwin Michael, J. B.

Fishburn, Lucian H. Cocke, and Mrs. S. H. McVitty of Salem. Out-of-town members included the Reverend Charles F. Myers of Greensboro, North Carolina, the Reverend Sparks W. Melton of Norfolk, Douglas S. Freeman of Richmond, and Ben E. Geer of Greenville, South Carolina.

In April 1927 the alumnae held the great spring pilgrimage to inaugurate the first major endowment campaign. Needed for minimum general endowment was $500,000, plus $150,000 for capital improvements. The alumnae pledged now $22,000, and the drive was launched. In June the local community acted: the Roanoke newspaper of June 17 headlined the "Flying Squadron of 48 Business Men to Solicit in the City"—within the week they secured pledges totaling $145,393. From there the drive spread over the country. In February 1930, the Association of American Colleges elected Hollins to its membership. The following year there was a tentative proposal to suggest Hollins as the woman's college to be coordinated with the University of Virginia, but Hollins refused the nomination.

The decisive step came on August 1, 1932, when Miss Matty Cocke handed the deed to Hollins College to David Denton Hull, president of the self-perpetuating board of a publicly owned college. Miss Matty's work was almost finished, and within a year she was to turn it over to her successor. Finally, in December 1932, Hollins was admitted to the Southern Association of Colleges and Secondary Schools, one of the most demanding of the accrediting agencies.

As a guide to the future there stood the statement of the purposes for which the Hollins College Corporation had been formed:

1. To conduct a college for the higher education of women, and for their instruction in the various branches of Literature, Science, and Art, and the education contemplated shall keep service as well as culture constantly in view.

2. While the presentation of the right ideals of character and conduct and the fostering of a religious spirit are included among the means necessary to the attainment of this object, no sectarian tests shall be required for membership on the Board of Trustees of the Corporation, the faculty or the student body.

PRESIDENT MATTY L. COCKE (Figs. 78, 79) Miss Matty, born Martha Louise Cocke in 1855, began her services to Hollins Institute as a child carrying candles to students' rooms each evening. Her formal education ended before she was nineteen, but in later years she received the honorary degrees of Doctor of Literature from the Woman's College of Richmond and of Doctor of Laws from Roanoke College.

What her Hollins girls were to appreciate and remember, wrote her grandniece Susanna Turner for the *Alumnae Quarterly* in 1938, was that "her very presence taught students and faculty alike a way of life. . . . She gave new encouragement from her own quiet wisdom, her dignity, and her all-pervading faith."

The practice of singing to Miss Matty on her birthday, October 9, was begun in 1930 and continued in her memory after her death in 1938.

MARION ESTES COCKE (Fig. 80) "Mr. Estes" appears in the photograph as he looked when he first worked for Hollins. He was to serve the college for fifty-five years under four presidents. Indeed, Mr. Estes, born at Hollins in 1876, took successively and often simultaneously varied roles; if any dominated, they were related to the strengthening of the academic quality of the college.

He returned to Hollins after securing B.A. and M.A. degrees from the University of Virginia and for some years taught physics, mathematics, and chemistry. He then added the duties of academic dean and later those of vice-president. In this latter capacity he directed the admissions office and also engaged preachers, lecturers, and artists, as well as taking an active part in appointing new instructors. He was for a long time treasurer and financial adviser to the president. He worked actively to have Hollins accredited by the Southern Association and served as president of the Virginia Association of Colleges.

When Mr. Estes retired in 1952, the board expressed appreciation "for his wise and kindly leadership, for his gentlemanly good nature and disposition that have won many friends for Hollins." Students remember, also, his jovial participating in extracurricular events and the warm hospitality dispensed by Mr. Estes and his wife in their campus home.

JOSEPH A. TURNER (Fig. 81) "To thousands of alumnae and friends of Hollins College all over the land," said the newspaper obituary after his death in 1937, "Joe Turner typified the spirit of Hollins—genial, friendly, cultured and devoted to the best things, not only in education, but in social, civic, political, and religious walks of life. To him the college owes much, the alumnae more, and the community most of all."

Joseph A. Turner was born on the Hollins campus in 1875, and after graduating from Richmond College and the University of Virginia, returned to devote his life to building what he called "the greater Hollins." He supervised construction of the new buildings; he built up the herd and the dairy; he took charge of the endowment campaign; he worked closely with students in everything from sports to benefits. He worked, too, with civic welfare in city and county, on the county board of supervisors, in the public schools, with the Rotary Club, as director of the Virginia Good Roads Association, on the board of Virginia Polytechnic Institute. Joe Turner also was a fine historian, charter member and president of the Southwest Virginia Historical Society, and inaugurator of the first systematic collecting of archives for the history of Hollins.

HOLLINS HERD (Fig. 82) Long a feature of the landscape were the Holstein-Friesian cows of the Hollins herd, started in 1907. There were also beef cattle and horses, pigs and sheep, and a vineyard, an apple orchard, and vegetable gardens.

Traditionally all cows bore names beginning with *H*—Hansel, Hazard, Hamlet, Hobo, Harlequin. Having won an impressive line of awards, particularly under long-term farm manager Aubrey Drewry, they were finally given up in 1968. But still after that time beef cattle were occasionally brought in to graze on the Hollins pastures.

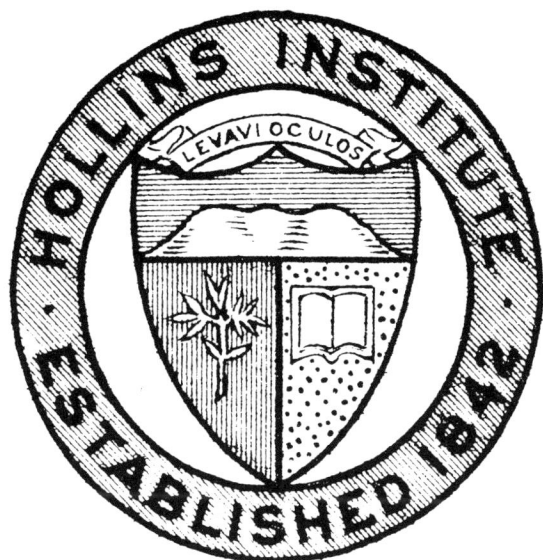

OFFICIAL SEALS (Figs. 83, 84) A new seal for Hollins Institute was designed in 1901 by Dr. J. M. McBryde of the English Department and Joe Turner. Within a circular frame was a shield bearing in the upper half a profile of Tinker Mountain and in its two quarters below a book on a gold ground, signifying knowledge, and a lily on red, symbolizing purity. The motto, *Levavi Oculos,* was taken from Psalm 121: "I will lift up mine eyes unto the hills."

The internal design was changed in 1909 to the one still in use, and in 1911, after the institute became a college, the frame became oval. The chevron dividing the area of this seal, according to heraldry, suggests the roof of a house, and was given to younger sons to indicate their independence. The three fleurs-de-lys that replaced the lily typify both purity and regality. The gold background—indicated on un-colored seals by dots—behind the book implies highest achievement; horizontal lines indicate blue sky behind the mountain.

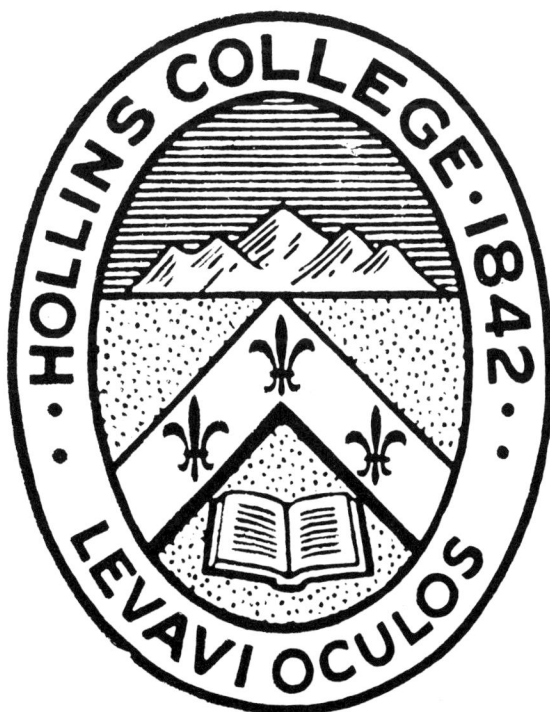

ERICH RATH AND THE CHOIR (Figs. 85, 86) Erich Rath, a young German musician, arrived in 1891 to start his teaching in this country. Except for a few years spent in Washington, he stayed at Hollins until his retirement in 1936, acting as head of the music department from 1907 on. He married Leila Turner, granddaughter of Charles Lewis Cocke; she taught German for many years.

Rath greatly expanded and strengthened the music offerings through the B.M. degree. He encouraged the composing of original music and built up the choral club and choir. The choir began to travel in the late 1920s, first through Virginia, and then to sing at a meeting of the National Music Federation in Boston.

Hollins alumnae remember Professor Rath with much affection as one of their most loved and respected teachers. After his retirement he wrote a biographical essay, "Vannie's Memoirs," which is of considerable interest for its personal notes on Hollins history.

RATH HAUS (Fig. 87) Rath Haus, the home of "Vannie" and "Mun-nie" Rath, as they were affectionately called, was the first of the houses to be built for faculty, the first home to have a Christmas tree, and always a place where students were cordially entertained. Built in 1907, it was placed between the old Music and Art Hall and the older Teach-ers' Cottage, which had been erected in 1885 as a small residence by a parent, Mrs. L. V. Kapp, and altered from time to time. Rath Haus, after serving as faculty residence and then as student dormitory, be-came in the fall of 1970 an informal student center, serving pizza and the first licensed beer to be sold on campus.

MARIA S. PARKINSON (Fig. 88) Maria S. Parkinson, niece of Charles Lewis Cocke, was born in New Kent County, Virginia, in 1858. She was educated at Hollins Institute from 1872 to 1877 and then spent several years at Vassar. In 1897 Charles Lewis appointed her lady principal of the institute, a title which she held until 1921. From 1921 to 1924 she was social director, and after her retirement resided in the alumnae Tea House. After her death in Richmond in 1946, she was buried in the family cemetery at Hollins.

An editorial in the Roanoke newspaper characterized Miss Parkinson as a "cultured gentlewoman whose contacts with the girls for more than a quarter of a century were marked by innate dignity and gracious charm." It was she who initiated the celebration of Founder's Day, and who is remembered for a happy combination of intellectual discussion and afternoon tea. Many students and faculty have vivid memories, too, of their trips to Europe with Miss Parkinson. She conducted some thirty such tours in grand style.

89.   First Freya May Day, 1903

FREYA MAY DAY (Fig. 89) A group of students got together in 1902 to revive the moribund May Day festivities. As charter members of the Fairies of Freya, they put on their first production the following spring and sponsored May Day for some decades. Often the characters were masked, especially in the early years, as befitting the secrecy of the society, and the symbol of the Freya bird was prominently displayed over the queen's throne. Original plays, pantomimes, dances, and music were composed. The college song, *The Green and the Gold,* with words by Phoebe Hunter and music by Almah Stuart McConihay, was first sung on May Day, 1909.

91. Fairies, 1915

OTHER MAY DAYS (Figs. 90–93) Some notable later May Days included that of 1911, with its relevant play, *My Wife Is a Suffragette;* the patriotic production of 1914, attended by Vice-President Thomas R. Marshall, Mr. and Mrs. Sinclair Lewis, and Senator and Mrs. Kern from Indiana; and the *Pilgrims to Canterbury* show of 1928 (Freya's twenty-fifth anniversary), which incorporated a miracle play of Cain and Abel performed on a pageant wagon in true medieval fashion.

92. Miss Matty and Vice-President Marshall, 1914 May Day

90. Queen and attendants, 1913

94. May Day in the Forest of Arden, 1910

FOREST OF ARDEN (Fig. 94) Hollins's own Forest of Arden was named by the celebrated Shakespearean actor Sir Philip Ben Greet, who came to Hollins on tour in 1907 to present *As You Like It*. Finding a natural stage in the grove of walnuts, oaks, and hickories near the sulphur spring, he dubbed it the Forest of Arden. The Ben Greet Players returned several times between 1907 and 1931, when they gave *Macbeth* in the new theater. Accompanying them in 1909 was Katherine Boyce Tupper, Hollins '02 (Mrs. George C. Marshall), playing Katharina and Ophelia.

93. Angels and devils on pageant wagon, 1928

LITTLE MAY DAY (Figs. 95, 96) A Little May Day was put on by faculty children enrolled in "Peyton University," founded by Miss Bessie Peyton in 1907. College girls later transformed this early morning frolic into Nixie-Pixie May Day, and wheeled their queens around the quadrangle while singing the children's ditty

> Oh, we have the best of times
> Every one agrees
> Little Nixie-Pixie folk
> Helping to grow the trees, the trees, the trees.

A wheelbarrow replaced the children's pony cart, and some imaginative playing with headgear in a play production class of 1935 led to the custom of choosing as queen the girl under the most ridiculous hat.

95. Little May Day, 1914

96. Nixie-Pixie Queen, 1945

97. Class Day, 1905: girls with willow chain

98. Founder's Day stunt, class of 1914

CLASS DAY (Fig. 97) Senior Class Day, preceding commencement, featured graduates bearing garlands of willow, of honeysuckle and roses, or of daisies. Centered in the class of 1905 is the future Hollins president, Bessie Carter Randolph. Occasionally sophomores were also festooned, and from 1909 on they prepared the daisy chain to be passed on to the seniors at the close of the ceremonies. It was then draped over the lawn in the outline of the class numerals.

99.   Procession to cemetery, 1933

FOUNDER'S DAY (Figs. 98, 99) Founder's Day in the early years of Miss Matty's presidency was a great holiday. There was usually a convocation the night before, with a speaker on the history and traditions of Hollins. Then, during the night, the classes vied to place a banner on the tall flagstaff topping the West Building cupola, until the cupola was removed in 1913. Class stunts continued through the day itself: in 1918, for example, stunts at dinner, at 3:00 P.M. in the gym, and after supper. Open house was held in the dorms, and a reception in the parlor, along with a convocation in the morning and a play at night. For Founder's Day of 1920, Miss Loulie A. Snead, teacher of English, wrote the hymn, *Where Are the Dreams of the Dreamer?*, traditionally sung thereafter.

By the 1930s, however, solemnity was the rule, with the senior class processing in cap and gown to the Cocke family cemetery on the hill, where they placed a wreath on the founder's grave.

100. Miss Matty breaks ground for library

101. Entrance portico, library

COCKE MEMORIAL LIBRARY (Figs. 100–104) Shortly after Cocke's death a memorial fund was begun for a new library. It took seven years and almost $19,000 to get one, but finally the cornerstone was laid on June 2, 1908, in a ceremony conducted by the Order of Masons in full regalia. The formal opening took place on December 2. "Student body, faculty, and speakers marched across campus to strains of the overture 'Light Cavalry' by Suppé," reported the *Quarterly,* to attend the program in the combined gymnasium–auditorium on the ground floor and the receptions in upper rooms.

The central hall was adorned with the 1890 portrait of Charles Lewis, others of Susanna and "Uncle Billy" Pleasants, and the mahogany grandfather clock given by the faculty. On the top floor were two large rooms for Euzelians and Euepians and smaller offices for *Spinster* and *Quarterly* staffs.

The new library was designed by architects Frye and Chesterman with an Ionic portico facing that of Main. In style it reflected early twentieth-century eclecticism: proportions and trim echoed varied late Georgian or Federal patterns then generally termed colonial. The building rose steeply; in later years librarian Dorothy Doerr was to advertise for student helpers with the agility of mountain goats. But it was given breadth within the year by the addition of covered colonnades that made explicit the now cloistered quadrangle.

102. Central hall, library

103. Reading room, 1937

104. Gymnasium-auditorium, library

SENIOR BONFIRE (Fig. 105) The commencement concert in the evening was followed by the bonfire at the library steps. In early years, seniors burned their books and notes, but soon they shifted to symbolic destruction. The photograph shows a reenactment of the bonfire for the Spring Pilgrimage of 1927. Students on the left wore costumes from 1842.

SUSANNA INFIRMARY (Fig. 106) The new infirmary named in honor of Mrs. Cocke and designed by Frye and Chesterman was built during the summer of 1910. It also copied late Georgian or Federal details: corner quoins, accented central portion, smaller upper story, and elliptical ornament. It marked the first step toward the formation of a new quadrangle that was later to be developed toward the southeast, where now stood stables, the carpenter's shop, and other maintenance buildings.

NEW BRIDGE AND BEALE MEMORIAL GARDEN (Figs. 107, 108)
The old bridge over the lower area behind the Memorial Library
(where vegetable gardens had once flourished) had been replaced by
a new one in 1908, and this area, with its little brook, became an even
more popular recreation ground. It was formalized with a beautifully
landscaped garden planned by A. A. Farnham in 1930: the Lucy
Preston Beale Memorial Garden given by her daughter, Mrs. Oscar C.
Huffman. Both mother and daughter were Hollins alumnae.

Increasingly the entrance to the campus was gaining color and design. In 1918, honoring his alumnae daughters, Evelyn and Louise,
Mr. J. B. Fishburn of Roanoke had given a new entrance gate, designed by Frye and Stone of colonial brick trimmed with limestone.
Successive graduating classes were to plant flowering fruit trees on the
rise behind the Memorial Garden.

109. Student government officers in *Spinster,* 1913

110. Freshmen, 1911

STUDENT GOVERNMENT (Figs. 109–112) As early as 1903 the proctor system had given way to an honor code, and there were sporadic attempts to organize a Student Body from 1904 on. By 1913–14, when mention of it first appeared in the catalogue, the student government was firmly established under its president, Marguerite Hearsey. Its aim, stated in the 1917–18 catalogue, was to foster "freedom for the development of the individual interest and character consistent with good order and decorum necessary for the progress of college work."

Hollins was host in 1919 to representatives from almost thirty colleges for the Southern Intercollegiate Association of Student Government. Then in 1920 emerged the student forum, made up of heads of all organizations. The first open forum was held in May of 1921 to discuss two major issues. One was whether to hold intercollegiate debates with Agnes Scott, Randolph Macon, and Sophie Newcomb; this met with a favorable response. The other issue was the perennial one of dress: whether one might wear short skirts, rolled hose, extreme hairdress, and French heels in laboratory classes. The decision was for moderation.

Judicial and executive councils existed early, but not until the fall of 1928 was a joint legislative committee instituted. At that time two students began publication of a newspaper, the *Hollins Student Life,* in addition to the *Magazine* which the Student Association had taken over in 1916 from the fading Euzelian and Euepian literary societies.

111. Sophomores, 1920

112. Members of Phi Mu Sorority, 1929

113.   Cotillion in library basement, 1920

STUDENT ORGANIZATIONS (Figs. 113–115) The *Spinster* of 1910 pictures five organizations (Student Body, YWCA, Euzelian, Euepian, Hollins *Quarterly*), three athletic clubs (tennis, Yemassee, Mohican), and forty-three others, primarily social. Many of these continued into the following decade, even though gently lampooned, as in the 1913 *Spinster:*

> Hollins's climate seems to favor
> Rapid mushrooms growing;
> For daily there are springing up
> Clubs beyond all knowing.

There were the Clubs We Are Born To—some dozen or more, of various states, of Yankees, and of foreign students—and the Clubs We Have Achieved—Cotillion, the self-perpetuating honor society of Freya, Maskers and the Dramatic Society, the Glee Club, and the zany A.D.A., wearers of purple on Tuesdays, which began in 1907.

But by 1930 there was a marked change. Sororities, literary societies, Yemassees, and Mohicans were gone, and athletics and beauty sections had taken over.

114. Cotillion Club page in *Spinster,* 1927

115. Dramatic Club, 1912

116.   Chafing Dish Club, 1900

117.   Midnight Scholars, 1911

SUPPER CLUBS (Figs. 116, 117) Supper clubs flourished at Hollins as they did everywhere in the early twentieth century. Popular names included Night Hawks, Midnight Scholars, Epicureans, Ten Little Mice, Nine Naughty Nibblers, Eta Hunka Pi, and High Livers. It was a severe blow when chafing dishes with their possibly incendiary alcohol lamps were forbidden in 1907. A "Lament: Upon the Banishment of Chafing Dishes," appearing in the *Quarterly,* mourns that "the light of the alcohol lamp hath gone out," and sighs for the "pompadours withered and fallen"—hair curlers could no longer be heated.

NATIONAL SORORITIES (Fig. 118) Varied chapters of Greek-letter societies lasted a little over twenty-five years at Hollins. National sororities that existed in 1929, when they were abolished through choice of their members and overwhelming vote against them by the freshmen, were Kappa Delta, Phi Mu, Delta Delta Delta, Gamma Phi Beta, Pi Beta Phi, Chi Omega, and Zeta Tau Alpha.

118.   Tri Deltas, 1920

KELLER (Fig. 119) In the fall of 1909 a recreation room with kitchen was opened in the basement of Main Building, which had once been the dining room. This Keller was the first informal gathering place and appreciated for decades. In 1910 the first senior-class banquet was held here, following the bonfire and starting another tradition that was to continue for some time, even if carrying one's four-year roommate around the room was a bit strenuous. Held here were also some of the Cotillion dances, the A.D.A. skits, and various other events, such as the Hollins Pantry operated on Saturday nights by sophomores in 1930, with "fruit for those in training."

MARY WILLIAMSON (Fig. 120) Mary Williamson, graduate of Hollins Institute in 1897, began teaching English there in 1902. In 1912 she had a year's leave to study philosophy at Columbia University, and returned with an M.A. to teach philosophy at Hollins College until her retirement in 1947. From 1925 until 1934 she also served as dean. She is vividly characterized in the eulogy written by Virginia Moore, Hollins '23, in 1961: "A small, intense woman . . . with a manner direct, downright. . . . Sometimes, even in casual conversation, her special quality blazed out: a mind strong, alert, utterly unsentimental, joined to a moral sense devoted to distinctions between right and wrong; to character. . . . And people, people first and foremost, people overwhelmingly. Mary Williamson had a talent for fellowship. . . . Because Hollins at its best was an interpenetration of head and heart, she came to seem the very Hollins."

86

PLEASANTS SCIENCE HALL (Figs. 121, 122) Estes Cocke worked closely with the architects Frye and Chesterman for a proper science building to house the laboratories crowded into East and West buildings, and one finally materialized in 1914. It cost $60,000 and was dedicated to "Uncle Billy" Pleasants. Ground was broken on March 14, with earth spaded first by Charles Lewis Cocke III and then by the head of every department the building was to house: chemistry, biology, physics, astronomy, psychology, mathematics, and (temporarily) domestic science and art.

It was placed to extend north, balancing the infirmary, and again was of eclectic Colonial style. For its time, facilities were admirable. The laboratories were patterned after those of Columbia University, and there was a special observatory on the roof for the class in uranography. A room was set aside in the center of the second floor as a museum for southwest Virginian bird, plant, and animal life. And, reported the *Magazine* with glee, "shooting from the first to the fourth floor in the heart of the new Science Hall is the Hollins elevator!"

The April faculty meeting in Pleasants in 1925 disbanded abruptly when explosions rocked the building. Chemicals had been ignited by lightning and fire gutted the interior, but fortunately the exterior walls and brick partitions through the first two floors were undamaged, and the interior was rebuilt that summer.

122.   Pleasants after the fire, 1925

SHAKESPEARE TERCENTENARY (Figs. 123–125) In 1909 Hollins celebrated the centenary of Edgar Allan Poe, in 1912 that Dickins. But the greatest of all pageants was that composed for the tercentenary of Shakespeare's death by Miss Loulie A. Snead of the English department and presented on May 13, 1916. Its theme was "An Unrecorded Progress of Queen Elizabeth" to the Forest of Arden, to honor Master William Shakespeare. The pageant with its milkmaids and yokels, its explorers headed by Sir Francis Drake, its foresters and morris dancers, and all other varieties of Elizabethan folk, moved across campus to strains of seventeenth-century music, presenting as part of its afternoon revels excerpts from *Twelfth Night, As You Like It, Hamlet,* and the *Taming of the Shrew.*

Miss Matty played Queen Elizabeth; Estes Cocke was Master Shakespeare; some 800 supporting characters came from Hollins and from Roanoke and Salem schools and clubs. Special trains were run from Roanoke to Hollins, and there was an audience of more than 2,000. And again Hollins's Shakespeareana gained notice abroad, for a long article on the pageant was published in the Stratford-on-Avon *Herald.*

123.   Miss Matty as Queen Elizabeth

124. Shakespearean procession

125. The festival on front campus

WORLD WAR I (Fig. 126) The *Spinster* of 1919 was dedicated to the Red Cross and was completely a war issue, with war poems, flag borders, reports of college war work, and accounts of alumnae in the service. One alumna known to later generations of Hollins Abroaders was Sara P. Watson, who joined the YWCA overseas and remained to manage the Foyer Internationale des Etudiantes in Paris from 1920 to 1959.

Girls at school knitted sweaters, took courses in first aid and home nursing, made surgical dressings for the Base Hospital of the University of Virginia, and enrolled for the military drill introduced as part of gym work in the spring of 1917. They also partook of limited food in the dining room, bought Baby Bonds, and contributed generously to the Student Friendship War Fund and the United War Work Campaign. Maud Booth of the Salvation Army and other speakers came, but because of the war the celebration of Hollins's seventy-fifth anniversary was canceled.

126. Red Cross First Aid, 1917

HOLLINS COLLEGE IN 1921 (Fig. 128) The aerial photograph shows how the campus had been expanded by 1921. In the area behind the chapel and East Building is the row of new or renovated faculty and staff homes. From the Music and Art Building there extend Rath Haus, built in 1907; Teacher's Cottage, enlarged in 1918 and renamed Sandusky; Rosehill, built in 1911 as a residence for the widowed Mrs. Charles Henry Cocke; and Malvern Hill, built in 1913 as a residence for the M. Estes Cockes and named after a colonial home of the Cocke family. Opposite these are Turner Lodge, built in 1913 for Joe Turner and his family, and the foundations for Duchouquet, a duplex apartment. The large barn shown at the left was about to come down, and already most of the new barns had been built at the western end of the grounds.

THE HOLLINS BUS (Fig. 127) In 1917 a new bus replaced the old wagon that had transported so many girls, and the *Spinster* heralded the modern conveyance:

> Gustavus with his spanking span no longer may be seen;
> Instead our dashing Charlie lords it o'er the Gold and Green
> Of the Hollins automobile bus, huge, shining, and serene.

129.   The Little Theatre

130.   Backstage in the theater

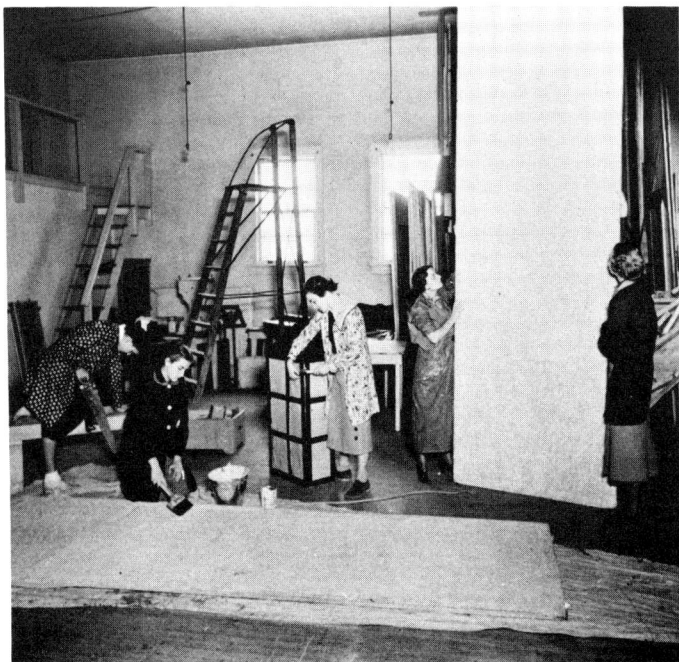

LITTLE THEATRE (Figs. 129, 130) Probably no new building at Hollins was ever more anticipated and appreciated by the students than was the Little Theatre, for it was in a very personal sense their own. A constant and absorbing interest in dramatic production finally brought them to the point where they could no longer endure the little stage and cramped audience area of the gymnasium–auditorium in the basement of the library. Just before Christmas vacation in 1922, then, a notice appeared on the bulletin board: "If you have the Hollins spirit come back after Christmas with a pledge of $30 or the $30." If 300 students pledged, there would be $9,000; hopefully, $10,000 would do it. Actually the idea had germinated months before, and the original plan was to have a building with gymnasium, including swimming pool, on the ground floor, and a theater above. But the scheme soon grew more ambitious and caught fire, intriguing administrators and alumnae as well. Students raised $45,000 toward the actual $65,000 cost of the Little Theatre, and by spring of 1924 it was ready.

The Little Theatre movement was just then at its height across the country, and the Hollins structure, built by the Roanoke firm of Frye and Stone, brought excitingly favorable comment. A long article in the *Little Theatre Monthly* of December 1924 described it as "the most perfectly designed and appointed playhouse in any college or university in America . . . with dimensions that shame those of more than one well-known professional theatre in New York."

131. *The Enchanted April,* 1933

PERFORMANCES (Fig. 131) The Little Theatre, with its 540 orchestra and 240 balcony seats, made it possible for Hollins to expand its community service and to become an active cultural center. Plays, lectures, recitals, operas, programs by symphony orchestras, succeeded each other in impressive variety. Wednesday nights from now on were designated for college convocations, which brought to Hollins outstanding speakers and performers and helped to dispel fears of insularity.

Hollins girls' special pleasure, however, was best voiced in the anticipatory lines in the 1922–23 Drama Board scrapbook: "*Our* Little Theatre! Won't it be fun acting on a stage which is big enough for us to give full sway to our emotions!" And for the official opening on May 31 the seniors presented Lord Dunsany's *If*—not yet released but given at Hollins by special permission.

CHRISTMAS CELEBRATIONS (Fig. 132) There were, early in the century, Christmas celebrations—M. Estelle Angier, Hollins '14, described in her diary a manger scene presented on the stage in the library basement, with livestock, donkey and sheep. By 1920 a service was held outdoors at night around a large community Christmas tree in the quadrangle, with a white candle shining from each dormitory window. In 1921 the students adopted the White Gift service initiated by the national YWCA. Gifts were symbolic ones such as loyalty or truth, and students dressed in white carried lighted candles.

During the 1920s a pageant was added to the service. Often it took the form of a medieval mystery or miracle play, presented on the library steps, and featuring as Madonna a student chosen by the Dramatic Board or Ye Merrie Masquers for her looks and character. There was some protest when both service and pageant were moved indoors after the Little Theatre was built.

132. Pageant with Madonna, 1927

FASHION SHOWS (Fig. 133) Fund-raising fashion shows were presented annually from 1921 on by the senior class, with modish apparel furnished by Roanoke dress shops: Samuel Spigel, B. Forman Sons, and S. H. Heironimus. This tradition has continued into the era of the miniskirt and the pants suit.

133. High fashion, 1929

134. Governor Harry S. Byrd at Hollins, 1929

VISITORS (Figs. 134–136) Hollins girls met many famous people: fathers like William Jennings Bryan, guests who returned frequently enough to become friends. Making initial visits in the prewar years were John Powell, Wilhelm Middelschulte, the Shubert and Mason string quartets, Mrs. Edward McDowell, and Edwin M. Poteat. From 1918 on came Sartell Prentice, Billy Sunday, John Erskine, Christian Gauss, Carter Glass, Douglas S. Freeman, and, often, the Devereux Players, the Letz Quartet, pianist Herma Menth, and scientist Gerald Wendt.

In 1924 Ida M. Tarbell spoke on women and Wilfrid Grenfell on Labrador, and Ruth Draper came twice. Following years brought Louis Réau, Morris G. Hindus, Carl Van Doren, Frederick Koch, and Rollo Walter Brown. Harlow Shapley and Reinhold Niebuhr made

the first of many visits. Pianists Leginska and Rudolph Reuter and organist T. Tertius Noble performed, as did such popular favorites as Tony Sarg's Marionettes and the Yale Puppeteers, the Don Cossack Chorus, Doris Niles and her dancers, and frequently the New York Theatre Guild and the Carolina Playmakers.

Governor Harry S. Byrd stopped for breakfast while inspecting airports in the fall of 1929. Brand Blanshard spoke in 1930. Then in 1931 came the memorable visit of Edwin Markham, and a talk by Edward L. Stone of Roanoke to accompany an exhibit of his superb collection of books. Finally, during Miss Matty's last year, came Cornelia Otis Skinner, pianists Bruce and Rosalind Simonds, Sherwood Eddy, and John H. Finley.

135. Edwin Markham with Annie Moomaw Schmelz

136. Exhibit of the Edward L. Stone Collection

TAYLOE GYMNASIUM (Figs. 137, 138) "Future Hollins women may look casually upon the gymnasium, but for the present it is impossible for us to do so," said *Cargoes* after the formal opening on November 17, 1924. Students were rightly proud of the tangible result of their endeavors, for the gym, like the theater, was their own. And the well-equipped structure, simple in design but harmonious with the others at Hollins, was marvellous after the makeshift gymnasia of East and West and Library basement. The opening program reflected the general glee, for "the real scream of the evening," said the morning news, "was the athletic wedding in which Gym joined Nasium in a state of perpetual motion, which is an athletic state followed by exhaustion."

The new building, designed by Frye and Stone and named in the early 1930s for Colonel Tayloe, began the framing of another quadrangle on back campus. Social activities also shifted in this direction. The first all-college dance with male escorts was held in the gym in March 1932, and followed by a pre-Christmas prom, to which faculty were invited; the *Hollins Student Life* announced that "the balcony is being reserved for them."

139. Tennis players, 1904

ATHLETICS (Figs. 139–141) Fencing became popular in 1904. The wearing of bloomers, permitted from 1913 on, allowed more freedom of action both in gym classes and in climbing Tinker; the uniform specified for gym included "black bloomers, all-white middy blouses, black athletic stockings and white tennis shoes."

The new gymnasium, however, brought an end to the Yemassee-Mohican rivalry, for basketball now became an indoor sport. A second hockey field was added to the old one of 1919, and the Thanksgiving game in 1924 inaugurated the contests between the Odd and Even hockey teams. A Fox Movietone feature included the Thanksgiving game, in a movie made in 1928—the same fall that the college newspaper happily announced the creation of a "real 3-hole golf course" on back campus.

140. Fencing team, 1904

141. Mohicans, 1918

FIRST HORSE SHOW (Fig. 142) For years the students clamored for horseback riding, and soon after it was permitted in the spring of 1930 Major C. O. Graves became riding master. The first Hollins horse show, held on May 9, 1931, was also the first one in the area, and followed within the year by shows in Salem, Bedford, and Blacksburg. Three classes in walk, trot, and canter were included, with two in jumping. The last event on the program was a gymkhana featuring egg-and-spoon, nightdress, and wheelbarrow races. The show had its exciting moments, as Leonora Alexander, president of the riding club, pointed out in her report for the *Alumnae Quarterly:* "There being no permanent ring, small pines were stuck in the ground to form a circle. These certainly did not take the place of a fence, however; not only did one horse run away with its rider, but also one of the outside entries left the ring and plunged his rider into Carvin Creek! . . . even Aunt Bess remarked on how well the girls fell!"

PRESSER MUSIC BUILDING (Figs. 143, 144) The third of the struc-
tures added to the campus in the mid-1920s was a happy gift. Theodore
Presser, member of the music faculty from 1880 to 1883, had gone on
to begin publication of the *Etude* magazine in Lynchburg and then to
establish the Presser Publishing Company in Philadelphia. His gift to
Hollins, announced on Founder's Day in 1925, was his first public
donation of a building.

Theodore Presser died before the building was finished, but James
Francis Cooke, president of the Presser Foundation, came to speak at
the formal dedication of the $56,000 structure on March 31, 1926,
and praised it as "the first of a long series of conservatory buildings"
to be furthered by the foundation. Indeed, the plan for the Hollins
music building, designed by Erich Rath, was to provide the model for
some of these. Studios, practice and class rooms, and an auditorium
seating two hundred people were fitted within an again neo-Colonial
framework, enhanced here by blind arcading and delicate Federal detail.

In 1971 a new music listening room was created in the former
auditorium and dedicated in honor of Erich Rath.

SPRING PILGRIMAGE (Fig. 145) On April 15, 1927, the alumnae began their three-day pilgrimage, sparking the first major endowment campaign. A highlight was the historical pageant of Hollins history from 1842 to 1927, augmented by sports, May Day, and a banquet attended by two hundred alumnae.

Colonel Tayloe and Charles and Susanna Cocke were portrayed by their grandchildren Tayloe Rogers, Mary Stuart Cocke Goodwin, and C. Francis Cocke. Lelia Cocke represented Miss Matty carrying candles to the dormitory rooms, and Virginia Williams took the role of Susan Williams, first winner of a full graduate diploma from the Female Seminary in 1856.

MAY QUEENS (Fig. 146) Six May queens illustrated fashion over a quarter of a century for the Spring Pilgrimage of 1927. Shown from left to right are Mrs. Leander Leigh, class of 1916, Mrs. W. H. Goodwin, 1906, Mrs. W. L. Tucker, 1921, Mrs. B. P. Chapman, 1912, Miss Elizabeth Charles Harmon, 1898, and Mrs. William C. Chaney, 1903.

EASTNOR (Figs. 147, 148) Eastnor, the president's house built in 1929, was named after the home of a branch of the Cocke family in Herfordshire, England. Miss Matty was photographed there serving tea from the silver service given to her by the alumnae on Founder's Day, 1934.

THE CABIN (Figs. 149, 150) Charles Lewis Cocke had recommended to the board in 1878 that the institute have "a farm and house to which pupils and teachers could retire occasionally for recreation and benefit to health." The trustees agreed "such an appendage" would be desirable, but they could not afford it. Now, in 1932, a cabin was built by the Athletic Association on a couple of acres of land purchased from the Walrond farm. Within walking distance from the college—about one and a half miles—this weekend outing spot added a great deal to Hollins recreation.

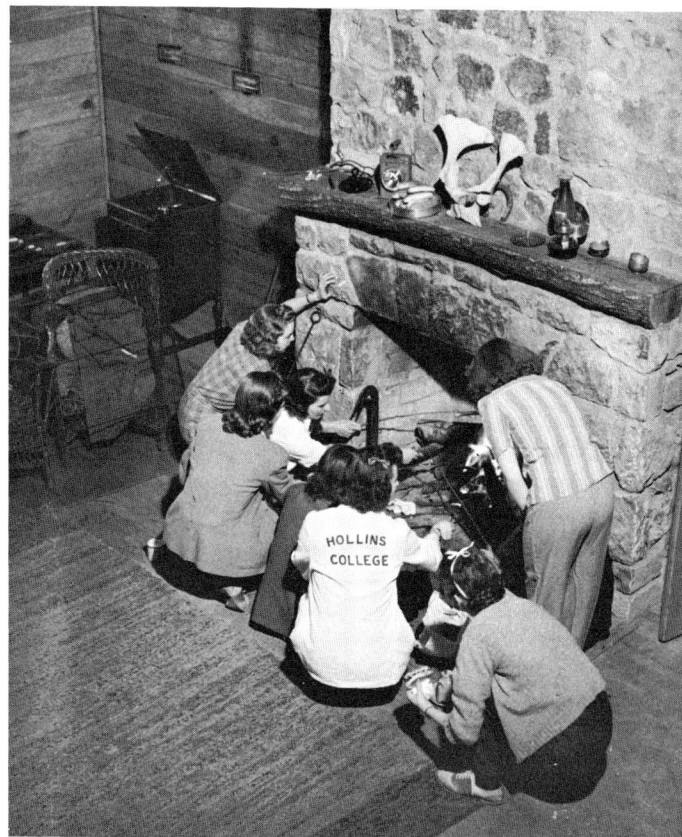

VI. Consolidation of the College

Miss Randolph's Presidency, 1933–1950

WE ARE RESOLVED," said President Randolph to the students at the opening of college in the fall of 1933, "students, faculty, and administration, to carry on the tradition of faithful and sincere intellectual endeavor at Hollins. In a time like this when economic strain and distress confuse educational values, we feel anew our responsibility to contribute fearless and clear thinking in our generation. In this endeavor, I shall rejoice in the best effort of every student."

The new president brought to Hollins an interest in scholarship and academic organization coupled with a firm belief in a solidly structured education for women, and she was to keep the college not only running but improving through years of nationwide depression and war. Already Bessie Carter Randolph, born in adjacent Botetourt County in 1885, was very familiar with Hollins's aims and problems, for she had received a Hollins A.B. degree in 1912 and remained to teach history until 1915. She became one of the alumnae representatives on the new board of trustees in 1927 and was active in subsequent planning.

Miss Randolph, however, brought to her new position much more than familiarity and understanding, for she had become an authority on international law and had gained varied educational experience. After receiving an M.A. from Radcliffe in 1916, she taught at Farmville State Teacher's College until 1920 and at Randolph-Macon Woman's College from 1921 to 1924. She then returned to Radcliffe, holding one of the five annual fellowships in international law given by the Carnegie Endowment for International Peace, and completed work for the Ph.D. in 1926. She went on to become professor of political science at Florida State College for Women, remaining there until she returned to Hollins as president.

The new administrator's board, faculty, and staff members must be complimented for their loyal service through these difficult years. Chairman of the board when Miss Randolph took office was David Denton Hull of Roanoke. Other members were Ben E. Geer of Greenville, South Carolina, Marion E. Park of Bryn Mawr, Mrs. S. H. McVitty

of Salem, and Charles I. Lunsford, E. Lee Trinkle, Junius P. Fishburn, J. B. Fishburn, C. Edwin Michael, W. C. Stephenson, and C. Francis Cocke of Roanoke. Cocke, grandson of the founder, succeeded Hull as chairman in 1938 and served in that position until 1968. Representatives of the Alumnae Association on Miss Randolph's first board were Marguerite C. Hearsey and Mary P. Singleton. Additions or replacements made to the board before World War II included Mrs. Brand Blanshard of Swarthmore, Henry W. Anderson of Richmond, John C. Metcalf of the University of Virginia, Pauline B. Williamson of New York City, Judge Alfred D. Barksdale of Lynchburg, George C. Peery of Tazewell, and Robert H. Smith, Mrs. Leonard G. Muse, Paul C. Buford, and L. J. Boxley of Roanoke. Miss Orlie Pell of New York was elected in 1943, Mrs. Alfred I. duPont of Wilmington in 1944, and Frank W. Rogers, LeRoy H. Smith, and Mrs. Barton W. Morris, all of Roanoke, in 1948–49. Alumnae representatives during these years (several were reappointed as regular board members) included Mrs. Howell B. Erminger, Jr., Emma M. Thom, Mrs. Milton R. Morgan, Mrs. J. E. Jackson, May D. Bush, Mrs. Stuart C. Campbell, Mrs. R. Finley Gayle, Mrs. Charles P. Orr, and Mrs. Jason B. Sowell.

By 1940 all the faculty who had worked under both Charles Lewis Cocke and Miss Matty were deceased or retired, save for Estes Cocke, who stayed on until 1952. But the group appointed by Miss Matty formed a strong nucleus for continuity through yet another decade or longer.

After Mary Williamson retired from the deanship in 1934, Marguerite Hearsey served as acting dean for a year, and Leslie Blanchard as dean from 1935 to 1939. Then Mary Phlegar Smith filled this administrative position, in which she was to be the mainstay of successive presidents until 1963. Miss Smith held a B.A. from the university in her home state of Pennsylvania and both M.A. and Ph.D. degrees from North Carolina. After experience gained at Bryn Mawr and Ohio University, she came to Hollins in 1932 to teach economics and sociology and by 1935 was named full professor.

President Randolph proved to be perspicacious in choosing new faculty who not only shared her desire for academic excellence but who were willing to work for low salaries, to live in the close situation on campus, and to share the common deprivations. Faculty and staff members who stayed to support the college were many. Appointed in the 1930s were Kathleen Jackson in economics, Paul Patterson in biology, Arthur Talmadge in music, John Ballator in art, Mary Vincent Long in English, Dorothy Doerr as librarian, and L. Aubrey Drewry as farm manager. Willard N. James came in 1940 to serve as secretary to the board and later as vice-president and treasurer. Before World War II came also Janet MacDonald in history and alumna Elizabeth Saunders Lee as college physician. During the war years, of course, with both men and women going into the services, there was considerable turnover, but staying on from those years were Frances Niederer in art and alumna Shirley Henn, who was first an assistant in the library and then efficiently performed multiple duties as executive secretary of the alumnae office. In the postwar years were appointed Helen Churchill in biology, alumna Anne McClenny in music, Herta Taussig Freitag in mathematics, and in 1949–50 Carolyn Moseley as freshman adviser and Ann Splitstone to fill the posts of registrar and director of admission.

Familiar long-term members of the Hollins staff through all or part of Miss Randolph's term of office also included administrative secretaries Lorna Denison and Helen Cobbs, cashier Barbara Hoge Cushing, and supervisor of buildings S. Frances Moore. Roy Obenchain served during these years as assistant to the dietitian. Ruth Crupper Reeves, Hollins '13, was for several years publicity secretary, and she was succeeded by Dorothy Scovil Vickery, who wrote the admirable history of Hollins published for the centennial celebration. Mrs. Irene Seguin managed the Tinker Tea House, Emily T. Slaydon succeeded Bessie Peyton as clerk of the new U.S. post office established at Hollins in 1934, and Mrs. Elizabeth Poulton and Mrs. Beatrice Oakley were on the social staff.

Particularly appreciated by members of the Hollins family were two benefits announced in 1946. One was a retirement annuity plan for faculty and certain other employees, begun on February 1 under contracts made with the Teachers Insurance and Annuity Association of America. The other was the Lalla Gresham Ball Fund established in memory of her mother by Mrs. duPont, with an initial gift of securities then worth close to $85,000. The annual income was to go toward faculty salaries.

About half of Miss Randolph's faculty held or acquired Ph.D.s, and they were increasingly productive in scholarly and creative work and active in professional societies as well as in the community. If Hollins is criticized for its low percentage of graduates through some of these years, it should also be praised for the high caliber of professional activity attained by many of those graduates. The faculty as a whole was also a liberal-minded group, and many individuals had very positive personalities. Faculty meetings, held monthly from 7:00 until 10:00 or 11:00 P.M., resembled old-fashioned town meetings (save for President Randolph's formal attire). Committee members were still appointed by the president, and there were only minor changes made in committees: for example, a new Academic Policy Committee resulted from the merger of the curriculum committee with that of admission, classifications, and schedule. In faculty meetings everything was discussed at length, and, since part of the time was given over to reports of professional activity, everyone knew what everyone else was doing.

President Randolph's first undertaking was the reorganization of the curriculum. She explained to the board why this was necessary, saying, "The traditional system (or lack of system) of independent or even sovereign departments is in general responsible in higher institutions for undue expense, overlapping of courses, sometimes interdepartmental rivalries to the great injury of the unlucky student, and for the artificial barriers between subjects closely related or identical." Through her first year in office she worked with the faculty on her new scheme, which was put into effect for the session of 1934–35.

Basic in the new divisional system were four general categories. Division I (humanities) embraced English, classical and modern languages, philosophy, and religion. Division II (social sciences) included history, political science, economics, sociology, and the one course then offered in education. Natural sciences and mathematics made up Division III, with biology, chemistry, physics, mathematics, and psychology. Division IV (fine arts) included art, music, and drama. Somewhere in limbo, but assured existence since they were required of all students, were hygiene and physical education.

Administratively this system created a hierarchic ladder. Prospective teachers progressed through interviews by departmental and divisional heads up to those by dean, vice-president, and president. Sanction for new courses had to be sought in a comparable sequence, ending with the total faculty. Students applying to major in a department had to be accepted by the division as well. The routine worked fairly smoothly, although it seemed to some faculty members exasperatingly multiple, and it did not wholly do away with departmental rivalries. But with a small faculty group, and with practically all its members living on campus and eating in the dining room, there was plenty of opportunity for interdivisional discussion.

Another feature of the new scheme was the sharp distinction made between the lower college, with its two years of required introductory courses, and the upper college, with advanced courses available only to those students who had ascended the ladder of prerequisites. There were few semester courses available, and actually electives were quite restricted. Each upperclassman had to fulfill requirements not only in her major but also in a related minor made up of advanced courses within the division. Graduates, then, had received a solid training within an area, even though some might have preferred the nineteenth-century elective and eclectic possibilities. Hollins had always been proud of the individual attention given to students, and now found virtue in the small classes of the upper college. In the 1930s the economics-sociology department instituted the seminar as a regular teaching device, and by 1940 made it a requirement for all its senior majors.

Basic aims of the college remained unchanged. Hollins remained nonsectarian but Christian in character and com-

mitted itself even more firmly to liberal arts education. Catalogues of the early years under President Randolph stated that the primary aim was "to give each student a sound, distinctly broad and humane education," adding, "every effort is directed toward the personal, intellectual, and moral development of the student." Faculty study then led to the formulating of a series of amplified statements which appeared in catalogues from 1948 to 1952, and indicate the ambitious optimism of the postwar educators. They read as follows:

To train the student to think, to discriminate, and to communicate.

To give a better understanding of the physical world, and of man's scientific, social, humanistic, and artistic development.

To offer each student sufficient specialization in one field, to develop and enrich her individual creative and scholarly talents, and to serve as a background for advanced study, vocations, or professional work.

To prepare for the intelligent and sensitive participation in the life of the family, the community, the nation, and the world.

To provide the conditions that promote mental and physical health; that foster individual integrity; that stimulate the desire to know and understand; and that maintain and strengthen spiritual values.

Majors were available in 1933–34 in Latin, English, philosophy, French, history, economics-sociology, biology, chemistry, physics-mathematics, psychology, art, and music (the B.M. in music was discontinued in 1934). To these were added in 1942 a Greek major, in 1945 a Spanish one, and in 1949 another combined major, history-political science.

There were other joint enterprises. In 1935 an interdepartmental course in social science was offered for freshmen, and in 1943 seven faculty members initiated an interdivisional course entitled Aesthetic Principles in the Contemporary Arts. In 1943 appeared also the first interdivisional major, in American studies, intended "to provide a better understanding of American culture for the more effective direction of life—especially in view of the reconstruction ahead." All of these possibilities were offered until the next major change of curriculum came in 1952.

Then for a few students there were junior years abroad, made available by other colleges or councils: in France from 1933 on, in Zurich from 1939. Such programs, naturally suspended during the war years, were reinstated in 1947.

By 1935 Hollins had finally been recognized by all accrediting agencies. In 1934 it was added to the college list of the American Association of Universities, and alumnae (retroactive to 1903) were admitted in 1935 to the American Association of University Women. Disheartening, however, was the fact that applications for a Phi Beta Kappa chapter were unsuccessful, in part for failings that could not be remedied. One of these was the fact that room and board remained part of faculty salaries, a situation economically necessary. More serious was the loss of students before graduation, and Hollins shared an apprehension felt by many women's colleges because of frighteningly high attrition.

This attrition, in fact, became a primary concern in the 1940s. Graduating classes had averaged about 44 during the first decade of President Randolph's tenure, and later often only a third of the entering students continued to graduation: 44 out of 135 in 1942; 51 out of 151 in 1944. But the president held firm to her course and stated the college's position for the alumnae in a 1943 *Bulletin*. She said: "The four-year program of the liberal arts college should . . . continue to be the normal and necessary course. . . . To the immediate winning of the war all higher institutions must dedicate all their resources, but they must not fail to prepare their students for the gigantic task of shaping a better world after the struggle ceases. The very existence of the liberal arts is one great objective for which this war is being waged throughout the earth." There was endless discussion about ways and means of holding students, but outside pressures were great and girls were restless. The major reasons for withdrawing from Hollins at the end of the sophomore year, said Dean Smith to the alumnae, were the desire for professional courses, the decision to transfer to universities nearer home, and matrimony.

The "war class" brightened the scene, for of 137 students who had entered Hollins in September 1941, 64 remained to receive B.A. degrees—the largest group as yet graduated from the college. But only 37 of the next class persisted, a most distressing low number, for as freshmen they had numbered 135 in a total enrollment of 326. Of these, 96 were from Virginia, 30 from North Carolina, 28 from West Virginia, 21 from New York, 13 each from New Jersey, South Carolina, and Texas, the rest scattered. Actually, there was no scarcity of students in the lower college, and at times Hollins was overcrowded. In 1946–47, for example, there were 376 students registered in contrast to the 329 of a decade earlier. But then enrollments dropped again. In Miss Randolph's last year, Hollins had 339 students and graduated only 57 of the 145 who had matriculated four years before. Regional proportions remained about the same, for there were then 100 Virginians among the 250 girls from southern states.

Existing buildings had to suffice during these decades, for very few more could be erected. In 1935 the old parsonage, built as a private home in 1888 and purchased by the college in 1923, was converted into faculty apartments. By 1936 a new apartment house, dedicated to Bessie Cocke Barbee, daughter of the founder, provided quarters for a few teachers and a living room used as a general faculty lounge. Then the alumnae, with a special fund-raising effort of their own, erected Tinker Tea House in 1939. Among essential facilities added to the campus were an enlarged power plant, a new milk pasteurization plant, provisions for water supply from the city of Roanoke, and a steam laundry to replace the former system of relying on laundresses in the "old field." Essential also was the rebuilding of the whole rear wall of East Building in 1945. But there were amenities added also: the refurbishing of dining hall and social rooms, and the extensive landscaping and planting of trees (some sixty elms, oaks, and dogwoods in 1939–40).

Even with major building impossible, President Randolph and her board showed foresight in realizing that a comprehensive plan for future expansion was essential if there were not to be haphazard growth of the campus. Such a plan was commissioned from W. Pope Barney of Philadelphia just before the war. Projected then were buildings calculated to accommodate a student body of five hundred, the number that contemporary studies indicated was most efficient for the administration of a small college. But war and postwar restrictions prevented the carrying out of even the first building in this admirable scheme. An Art Annex of cinder block and brick, quite unrelated to the overall plan, but expediently housing the art department and freeing its former space for other instruction, was joined to the rear of the Little Theatre in 1948. Even the completion of this building was delayed by lack of steel.

This era in the history of Hollins might well be characterized by the multiplicity—a plethora in the eyes of many— of required, all-college convocations. In the pretelevision days of the 1930s and 1940s renowned scholars, preachers, writers, actors, and musicians were available for modest honoraria, and even college deans and presidents had time for appearances at other institutions. If the rosters of names given in the pages below seem unduly long, alumnae and faculty will remember that they represent only a fraction of the total number of visitors. In fact, this surfeit of extracurricular learning occasioned constant protests from students, particularly in the postwar years.

Letters to *Hollins Columns* complained that other extracurricular activities were also overpowering, too many, and serving no real purpose. Yet students did not limit the number of their own collective burdens, as the elaborate point systems given in annual student handbooks indicate. Ten points (the maximum for any individual) were given to the offices of student government president or *Spinster* editor, but there were many lesser offices. Only 60 in all received points in 1939, but there were 84 in 1945 and 107 by 1949. The crux of the matter lay not in the number of activities but in the fact of compulsory attendance at class meetings, weekly student-government assemblies, chapel, or convoca-

tions. There were limited cuts available—two per semester for convocations—but they were also rationed; only ten seniors, for instance, might cut a given lecture. And although theoretically each student regulated her own class attendance, not all faculty understood the theory (they still had to tally absences daily and report them to the dean's office). Furthermore, there was a six-day week with two no-cut days before and after each holiday or examination period. At least one holiday was extended when President Randolph in her last year agreed to a Thanksgiving weekend.

There were also a great many social regulations. True, the students had come a long way from 1934, when they were allowed to ride in automobiles only with faculty or parents without special permission, to the late 1940s when they wanted to keep their own cars on campus. And by 1941 they were allowed to go elsewhere than the country club to dance (although this meant that the social staff had the onerous duty of checking roadhouses for an approved listing). Since Hollins girls went in large numbers to Lexington, Blacksburg, and Charlottesville, there were special rules and lodgings and chaperonage for those towns, which seemed illogical to girls whose friends were going to Princeton or Cornell. The breaking of minor social regulations put great stress on the honor system, which seemed to work quite well academically, because it was based on double reporting. This meant that each student was responsible not only for herself but for her peers, and many students could not assume such responsibility when it entailed reporting misconduct by their friends. As yet there was no great concern about propriety in dress. Students in gym outfits might cross front campus, say the handbooks of the thirties, "provided there is no loitering." A brief statement prohibited from 1937 on the wearing of socks after 7:00 P.M. and at all times in the dining room, drawing room, or in town. Students were expected to wear hats and gloves to Roanoke, and to dress for dinner.

Receptions and garden parties and formal banquets maintained a tradition of gracious hospitality. Hollins's first inaugural was held for President Randolph, and, despite the war, the grand celebration of the centennial was carried through. Students, thrown on their own resources particularly in the war years, went on with games and stunts and performances.

But increasingly the campus looked deserted on weekends, for Hollins girls were embracing the mobility now becoming characteristic of youth everywhere. They still traveled by train or bus, but with the opening of Roanoke's Woodrum Field in the fall of 1941 they began to take to the airways, rarely deterred by the need for parental permission to fly. By 1950 the image of the Hollins girl, and indeed that of Hollins College itself, was heading toward the transformation that was to come in the next era of the institution.

PRESIDENT BESSIE CARTER RANDOLPH (Fig. 151) At the close of President Randolph's term of office an article in the *Alumnae Quarterly* characterized her as having "a keen judicial mind, trained by long discipline to weigh and balance without emotion or prejudice the essential values in any conflicting group of issues," with a "fearless, incisive power of penetration to the core of the problem." But also noted were "her delightful humor and her whimsical charm in conversation." Many of her associates came to know and to appreciate all these qualities in their president. They realized, also, her encyclopedic knowledge, saw the stacks of newspapers and journals she read, enjoyed particularly the regional lore she so freely dispensed.

In addition to her work for Hollins, Miss Randolph held executive offices in the American Political Science Association, the American Society of International Law, and the Southern Council on International Relations. In the late 1930s she was the only woman member of the University of Virginia's Board of Visitors. She was also active in the American Association of University Women, serving as a member of its national committee on international relations and as chairman of its legislative program.

After her retirement in 1950, Miss Randolph resided in Lynchburg, where she died in 1966.

INSTALLATION OF PRESIDENT RANDOLPH (Fig. 152) The first presidential installation in Hollins history was held on the morning of Founder's Day, 1934. Dr. George Braxton Taylor, chaplain emeritus, gave the invocation, and the investiture was performed by David Denton Hull, chairman of the board. President Henry Noble McCracken of Vassar delivered his address to the Hollins family and ninety-two delegates from colleges, schools, educational associations, and scholarly societies. He spoke on "Three Values," saying that more important than the thing learned or the learner was the process of learning itself. Guests were then entertained at a reception and dinner, and watched an evening performance by students of *King Nutcracker,* with music by Tchaikovsky.

Appearing in the photograph with the new president are Mr. Hull, board members E. Lee Trinkle and Edwin Michael, President J. L. Jarman of the State Teacher's College at Farmville, Dr. McCracken, and Miss Matty Cocke.

CHARLES FRANCIS COCKE (Fig. 153) Hollins should honor equally with her Founder his grandson, C. Francis Cocke, who joined the board in 1929 and served as its chairman from 1938 to 1968, for his devotion to the college was constant and his contribution inestimable. A man of strength, wisdom, and charm, Cocke is remembered with esteem and affection. And no less notable than his contribution to Hollins was his activity in many other fields.

After graduating from the University of Virginia, Cocke studied law there, and was admitted to the bar in 1910. He continued his law practice after war years spent in the air service, and then went into banking, rising to the presidency of the American Bankers Association in 1951. His career also embraced the presidencies of the First National Exchange Bank of Roanoke, the Virginia State Library Board, the Roanoke Memorial Hospital Association, and the Virginia Bankers Association. He was a member of many boards, ranging through business, educational, and cultural fields.

From 1919 until 1961, Cocke served also as chancellor of the Episcopal Diocese of Southwestern Virginia, and after his retirement in 1964 he wrote several histories, three on Episcopal dioceses and one on St. Mark's Church in Fincastle.

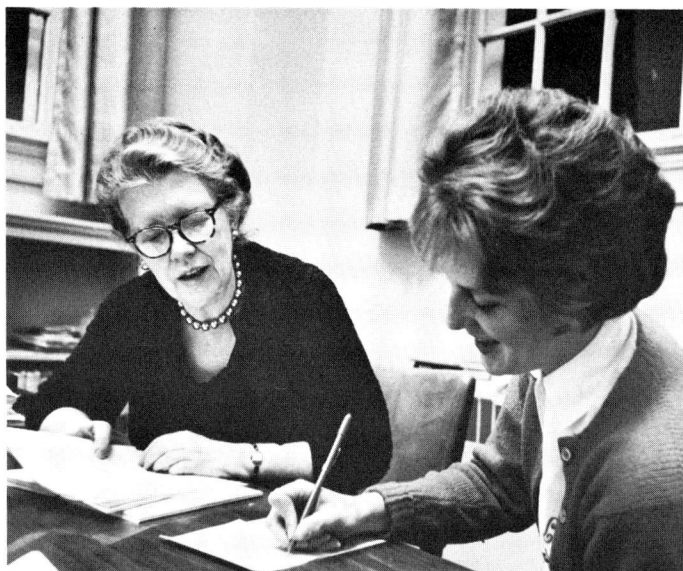

DEAN MARY PHLEGAR SMITH (Fig. 154) Dean Smith remarked in a chapel talk in her final year at Hollins that her aim had been "the furtherance of optimum conditions for intellectual progress." This she achieved, always with firmness combined with flexibility, and during her tenure there came many decisive changes. Outstanding was her gift for genuine rapport with students. Even with expanding numbers of Hollins girls, Dean Smith maintained her interest in each as an individual, fostering both academic and personal maturity and maintaining friendships long after graduation. Upon her retirement, Hollins College presented her with the honorary degree of Doctor of Humane Letters.

Dean Smith's influence also extended afield. For more than a decade she served on the board of trustees of Virginia Polytechnic Institute; in 1958 she became the first woman to chair the American Conference of Academic Deans; a few years later she was president of the Association of Virginia Colleges and a member of the Virginia Fulbright Committee. Meanwhile she was active in many state and local organizations, being, for example, on boards of the Roanoke Community Fund and the Mental Hygiene Service.

Her community service has continued since her retirement, as has her close contact with the college.

MARY LOUISE MADDREY (Fig. 155) When Miss Maddrey retired in 1959, her friend Professor Susie Blair commented that she probably knew more alumnae than did anyone else at Hollins. Many people other than alumnae, however, remember Miss Maddrey's gracious hospitality, her warm friendliness, and her public-spirited energy, all unfailing through her thirty-two years at Hollins.

Miss Maddrey, born in Hendersonville, North Carolina, was educated at the Woman's College of the state university. She came to Hollins in 1927, with a master's degree in Christian education from Columbia University and varied experience in guidance and personnel work, most recently at Christ Church House in New York City. At Hollins, as the first professionally trained head of the social office, she oversaw student housing, decorated rooms, and arranged all social affairs. She inaugurated the popular Christmas and examination period teas and did constant formal and informal advising.

She was active in the regional association of deans of women, and in community work as well, particularly with the AAUW and the Virginia Tuberculosis Association. She will long be remembered, also, for her devoted support of Mercy House.

CARNEGIE GIFTS (Fig. 156) Hollins was chosen as the one college in Virginia to receive the superb reference collections for art and music that the Carnegie Corporation gave to several institutions in 1933. For music there were 824 records with scores, 129 books, and a phonograph; for art, 170 books, 1,900 photographs, and several thousand slides. Terms of the grant required that these be housed apart from the college's main library; both were in Presser Building until the Art Annex was built in 1948.

157. The Stradivarius Quartet

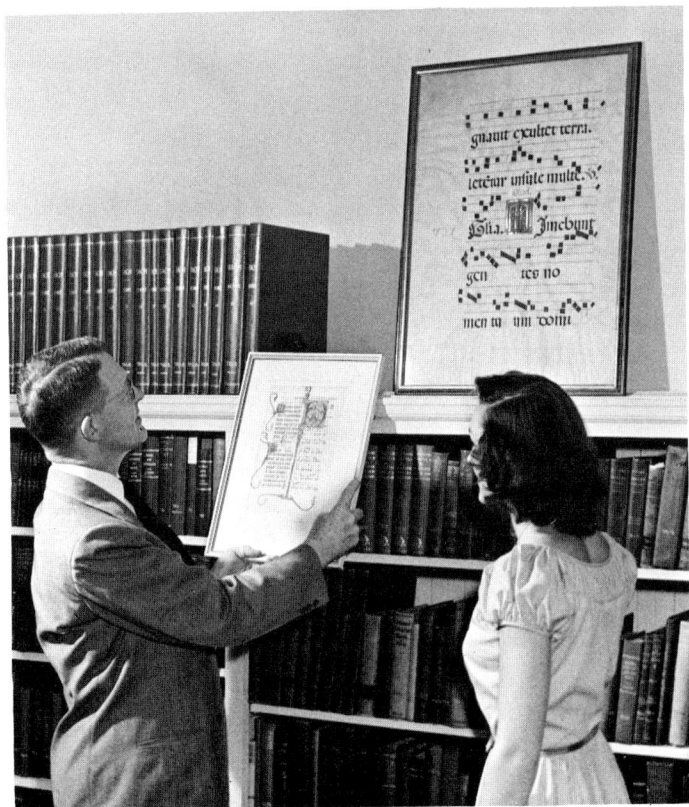

156. Professor Talmadge in Carnegie Music Library

MUSIC PROGRAMS (Figs. 157, 158) During President Randolph's tenure there was a richer series of musical programs than ever before or since. Professor Arthur Talmadge inaugurated the practice of bringing artists to Hollins for two-day visits; first of these, in 1937–38, were pianist Bruce Simonds and the members of the Stradivarius String Quartet. Hollins students had the opportunity, then, to become acquainted with such talented figures as pianists Rosalyn Tureck, Katherine Bacon, and Hugh Hodgson, organist Arthur Poister (who was to return as visiting professor in 1967–68), baritones Ernst Wolff and Yves Tinayre, and the Paganini and Belgian string quartets.

Among other performers who came during these years were pianist Maxim Schapiro; violinists Joseph Fuchs and Samuel Dushkin; organists Virgil Fox and André Marchal; the Budapest, London, Pascal, and Griller string quartets; singers Margaret Harshaw, Kathryn Meisle, John Jacob Niles, the Trapp Family Singers, Pierre Bernac accompanied by Francis Poulenc, and Hollins's own alumna opera star, Mary Curtis-Verna, '43.

In 1948 Hollins received the magnificent Sallie Gray Shepherd Fund of $50,000, given by Mrs. Malcolm Perkins, '08, in memory of her mother. Proceeds from this fund augmented the already well-established series of performances.

158. The Trapp Family Singers

CHAPEL CHOIR (Fig. 159) The choir sang now against the background of the new Aeolian-Skinner organ installed in Bradley Chapel in 1938 and dedicated to Erich Rath. New also was the Hollins College Chapel Choir series published by the Schirmer Music Company from 1942 on. Professor Talmadge composed some twenty works which were published during these decades, with more to come. The choir also began to travel more extensively and in 1949 began to produce joint programs with the Haverford College Choir. The highlight of the year, however, still remained the program for the White Gift service at Christmas.

MRS. ELEANOR ROOSEVELT (Figs. 161, 162) Mrs. Roosevelt paid a noon visit to the Hollins campus after her alumnae-sponsored talk in Roanoke in October 1938. She reported in her column, *My Day,* that Hollins reminded her of the University of Virginia and added: "I must say that the 350 girls I saw flitting around looked a very healthy, happy group."

ROBERT FROST (Fig. 160) Most popular of the poets who came to Hollins was Robert Frost, who was following the lecture circuit to many colleges in the thirties. Because he was a friend of Professor Janney (who had written articles on his poetry), Frost spent three days at Hollins in April 1937, with one evening given over to the Hollins Writers Club. Hollins girls, as always, were writing poetry of their own. By 1946 the college published its second anthology of *Hollins Verse,* compiled from poems written since the first anthology had appeared in 1930.

163. The Fillinger periodic table

164. Professor Patterson gathers mosses

SCIENTIFIC ACTIVITIES (Figs. 163, 164) Had it not been for Pearl Harbor, a *Life* magazine cover for December 1941 would have featured a photograph of Professor Fillinger's three-dimensional version of the Mendeleef periodic table. Instead it was published in the *Journal of Chemical Education* and included in the Virginia exhibit for the World's Fair. Chemistry students were joining Miss Fillinger in research, much of it pioneer work in colloid chemistry and chromatography; some were publishing articles or delivering papers for the Virginia Academy of Science. Professor Sitler's students were helping to build a Hollins collection of regional flora and fauna, and Professor Patterson's were working with him on bryophytes. Cognizance of "Dr. Pat's" mosses spread beyond Hollins, and in 1950 he was named one of America's forty eminent men of science.

Notable lecturers who came to Hollins before the war included George Washington Carver, Julian Huxley, and Robert Yerkes. In 1943 Bart J. Bok came from Harvard to speak on the four-hundredth anniversary of Copernicus's death. Then in the late 1940s came geneticist Lawrence H. Snyder, parapsychologist Joseph H. Rhine, and from Oak Ridge to explain the new nuclear developments, Ralph T. Overman and M. D. Peterson.

DINING ROOM (Fig. 165) Many alumnae will remember Botetourt Hall as it appeared when redecorated in 1935 by Mrs. McVitty, chairman of the buildings and grounds committee of the board. There were new mahogany tables and an inlaid seal under the dome, all brightened by a splendid chandelier given by Mrs. McVitty. Several alumnae joined her in donating screens with nostalgic scenes of old seminary and institute days.

In order to ensure general acquaintance and to maintain the family atmosphere, faculty and staff were still assigned to serve as heads of tables, with students rotating every few weeks.

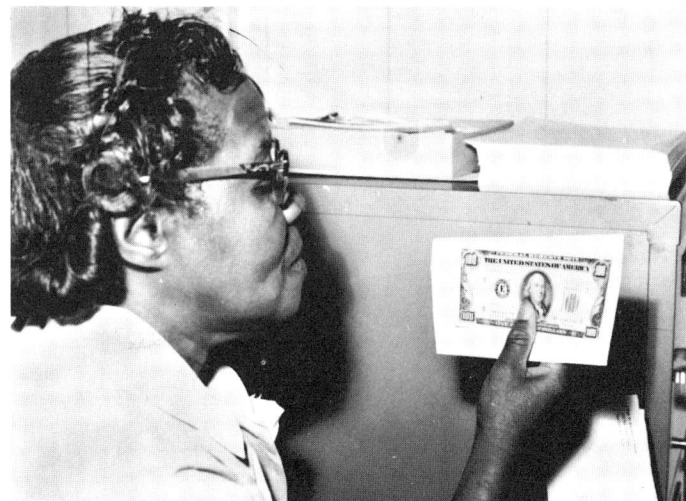

LEWIS AND MELISSA (Figs. 166, 167) Generations of students were called to meals by the triangle rung by Lewis Hunt, who for forty-seven years was head waiter in the dining room. As the *Alumnae Bulletin* remarked on his death in 1954, Lewis's "dignity was unassailable, his loyalty unquestioning, and his innate courtesy unfailing."

Generations also delighted in the good humor and sensible advice dispensed by Melissa Meade, who through a half-century assisted at a multitude of social functions and who continued her close connections with Hollins long after her retirement in 1964.

TINKER TEA HOUSE (Figs. 168, 169) Ground was broken by Maria F. Parkinson on August 17, 1939, for the Tinker Tea House, built by the alumnae and designed by Frye and Stone. On the ground floor of the $27,000 structure were fountain, dining rooms, and kitchen; upstairs were apartments and guest rooms. Its exterior landscaping was brightened with dogwood trees and shrubbery donated by board member Junius B. Fishburn.

Students were especially delighted with the fountain room and its corner "cracker store"; the *Quarterly* reported to the alumnae owners that "the students' highest compliment is that it looks like a smart hotel bar!" There was also music: for the opening "the nickelodeon turned over record after record."

170. Alumnae Institute, 1937

ALUMNAE INSTITUTES (Fig. 170) Summer institutes for alumnae
were offered annually from 1934 through 1937. Initially there were
two weeks of lectures by faculty on "Today's Point of View." In 1937
an ambitious program offered lectures by Gerhard Colm and Boris
Bogoslovsky of the New School for Social Research, Albert Coates of
the University of North Carolina's Institute of Government, alumna
philosopher Miriam McClammy, and G. Holmes Perkins, collaborator
with Walter Gropius at Harvard. Perkins, reported the *Alumnae
Quarterly,* "made gracious compliments about the lay-out at Hollins."
Susie Blair lectured on modern drama, and the Barter Players presented
Coward's *Private Lives* and Sherwood's *The Petrified Forest.*

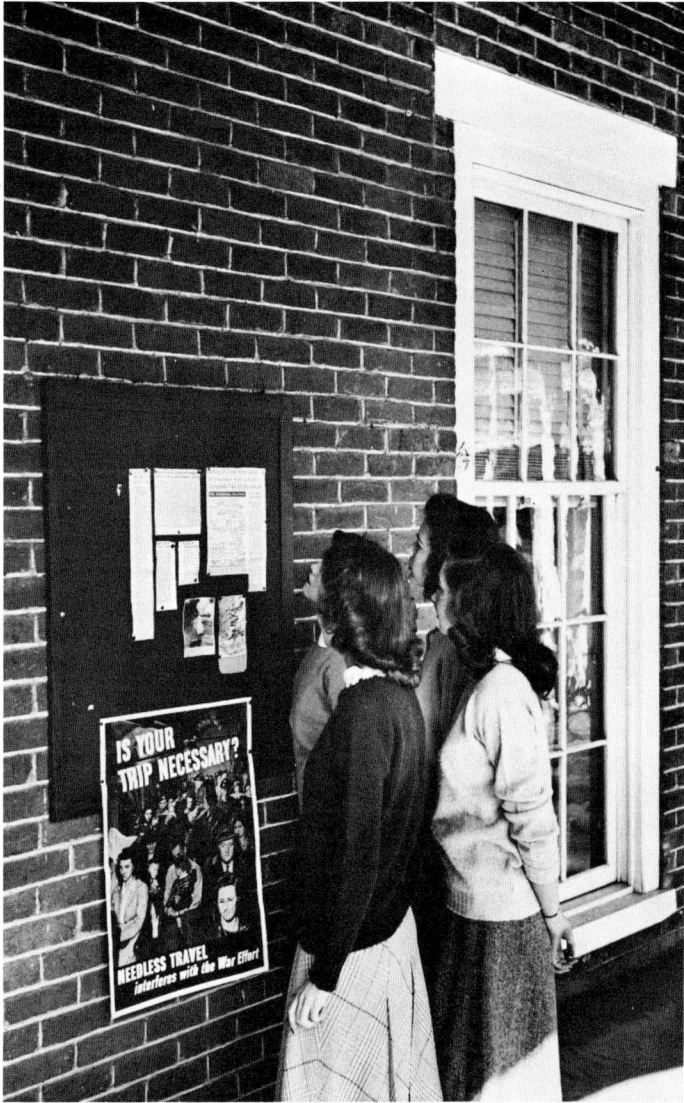

171.   Girls read I.R.C. bulletin board, 1943

Blanshard on pacifism. Hollins audiences heard about Germany from William E. Dodd, Erika Mann, and Nora Waln; about Russia from Maurice Hindus and Vera Micheles Dean; about the Arabian question from Philip Hitti; about the Far East from Hallett Abend and Freda Utley.

In the spring of 1945 Dr. Sarah Wambaugh, former adviser for the League of Nations, was appointed as the college's first week-long visiting lecturer. She was followed by Arthur Kuhn, who explained the Dumbarton Oaks proposals, and Clyde Eagleton, who talked about the United Nations. Hanson Baldwin lectured in 1946 on "The World of Tomorrow." In the late years of the decade, race problems were discussed by Benjamin E. Mays, and problems of law and government by Ellis Arnall, Colgate Darden, Gordon Blackwell, and William Yandell Elliot. In 1948 Charles A. Micaud came for two three-day seminars on foreign affairs.

INTERNATIONAL RELATIONS CLUB (Fig. 171) In 1934 the I.R.C., founded two years earlier, sponsored the first southern regional conference of the Women's League for Peace and Freedom, and delegates came from eighteen other colleges. Within a few years Hollins girls also met lecturers like Josephine Roche of the National Council for Prevention of War.

But as crises multiplied through the 1940s so did the complexity of international relations, and more and more experts came to explain, to interpret, or to predict. Commander Ellsburg of submarine *Squalus* fame (and Hollins father) spoke on "Defending America," and Brand

WORLD WAR II (Figs. 172, 173) To the blacked-out alerts, the courses in first aid, home nursing, physical fitness, and map making, the food rationing, and other often depressing activities or lack of activity of the war years, a welcome break came when students and faculty embarked on two weeks of apple picking for the Garland orchards in the fall of 1943. Thirty-one faculty members and 141 students energetically gathered 3,897 bushels of apples, helping the war effort by contributing their pay plus bonuses. Students also purchased an equipped ambulance for the armed services and took pride in the fact that Hollins was the first college in Virginia to receive a Red Cross College Unit. To aid the government in its transportation problem the college had a five-week Christmas vacation in 1942 (during which time each girl was expected to complete fifty hours of study) and eliminated the spring vacation. Again in 1944 there appeared a *War Spinster*.

174. General and Mrs. Marshall with M. Estes Cocke and C. Francis Cocke

175. Centennial ball

CENTENNIAL CELEBRATION (Figs. 174–178) The seventy-fifth anniversary of Hollins had not been celebrated because of one world war; now the hundredth fell during another. But this time, Hollins proceeded with the plans on which Professor Rachel Wilson's committee had been working for a year or more. Participating in the programs of May 17–19 were many guests already familiar with Hollins such as Frank Porter Graham, Harlow Shapley, John Dewey, Theodore H. Jack, Elizabeth Gilmore Holt, DeWitt Parker, and pianist John Powell. The Right Reverend Karl Block, Bishop of California, preached the sermon at the Centennial Service of Commemoration, and President Ada Louise Comstock of Radcliffe College gave the main address, "Women in This War." Panel discussions were held: "Liberty in America Today," "Morality and Religion in a Free Society," "The

Arts in a Free Society," and "Freedom of the Mind and Spirit." A personal and exciting note was added by the unexpected entrance of General George C. Marshall, Chief of Staff and husband of alumna Katherine Tupper, class of 1902.

Students dressed in costumes of the 1840s attended a centennial ball in a gymnasium transformed into an antebellum mansion, and there was a 100-year birthday cake.

177. John Dewey at garden party

178. Frank Porter Graham, Harlow Shapley, and Samuel A. Mitchell

176. President Randolph receives slice of birthday cake

179. Projected expansion plan, 1936

180. Plan of the Hollins campus, 1941

PROJECTED EXPANSION (Figs. 179–181) A tentative projection drawn for Joe Turner in 1936 by William Chester, art instructor, indicates that expansion of the campus toward the west was being considered. But architect W. Pope Barney in 1941 chose to group major buildings around the Beale Memorial Garden and to suggest future expansion toward the north. Barney was then chairman of the advisory board of architects for Princeton University and had had wide experience in college planning. Working closely with him at Hollins was Willard N. James.

The new plan was enthusiastically received when it was formally presented at the centennial celebration. It showed a new library on the low rise to the south, overlooking the garden, and smaller buildings for administration and fine arts flanking the Cocke Library (which was to be converted into classrooms). A new chapel was placed parallel to the theater, toward the east, and Turner Hall, the new dormitory, toward the west.

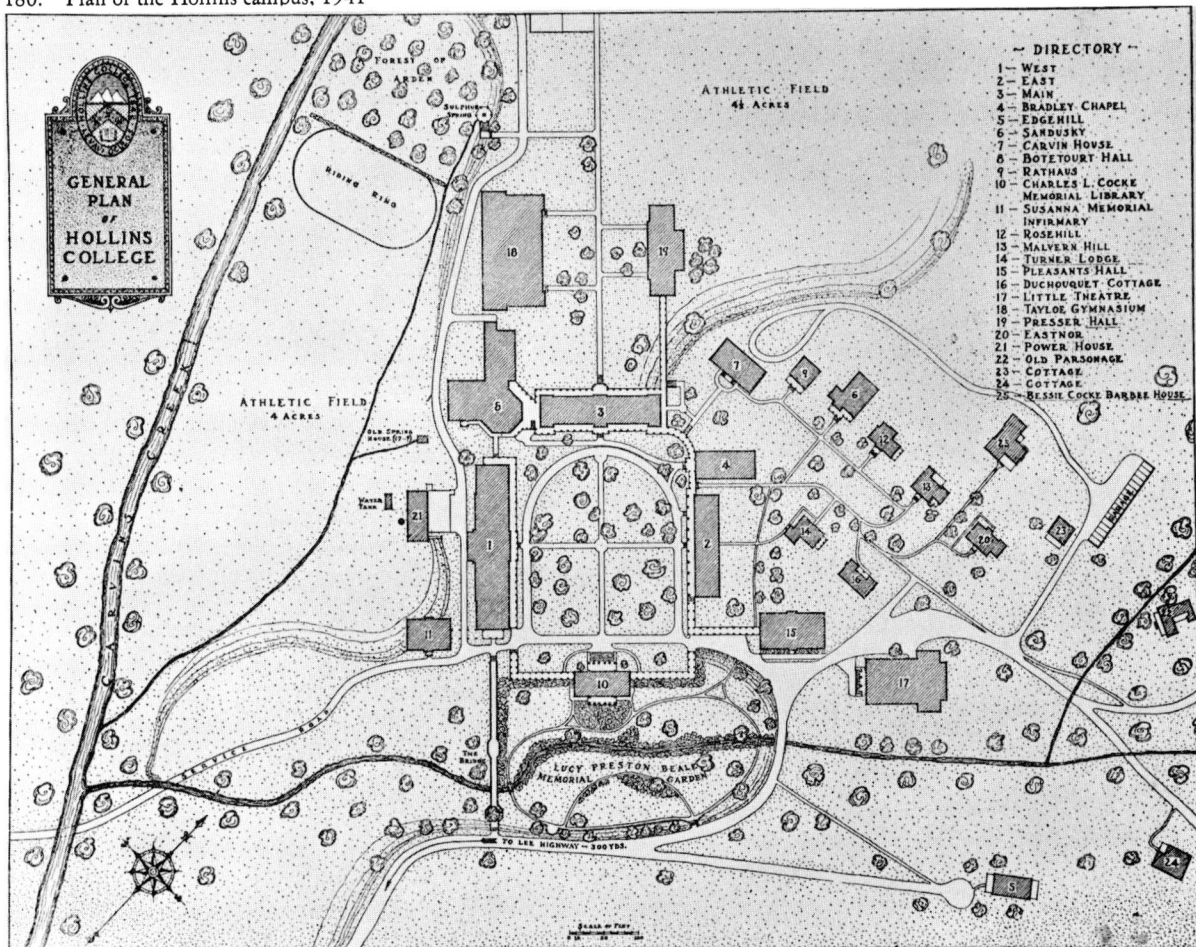

GENERAL PLAN of HOLLINS COLLEGE

DIRECTORY

1 — WEST
2 — EAST
3 — MAIN
4 — BRADLEY CHAPEL
5 — EDGEHILL
6 — SANDUSKY
7 — CARVIN HOUSE
8 — BOTETOURT HALL
9 — RATHAUS
10 — CHARLES L. COCKE MEMORIAL LIBRARY
11 — SUSANNA MEMORIAL INFIRMARY
12 — ROSEHILL
13 — MALVERN HILL
14 — TURNER LODGE
15 — PLEASANTS HALL
16 — DUCHOUQUET COTTAGE
17 — LITTLE THEATRE
18 — TAYLOE GYMNASIUM
19 — PRESSER HALL
20 — EASTNOR
21 — POWER HOUSE
22 — OLD PARSONAGE
23 — COTTAGE
24 — COTTAGE
25 — BESSIE COCKE BARBEE HOUSE

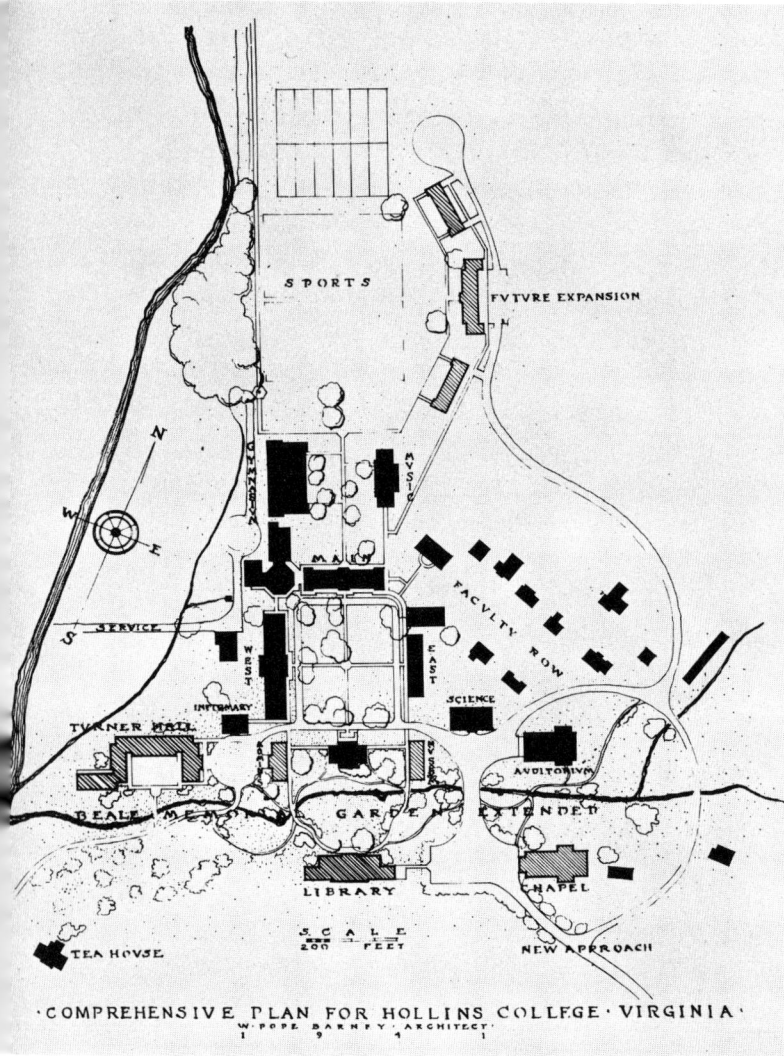

181. Plan with projected new buildings, 1941

PROJECTED TURNER HALL (Fig. 182) Preliminary plans for Turner Hall, which was to be built in stages, were authorized in 1945. But building for other than defense purposes was then impossible, and in 1946 a building permit was denied because Hollins was not included in the G.I. program. By the next year, estimated costs for Turner Hall had escalated from $350,000 to $500,000. When Turner Hall dormitory was finally built in 1952, the original plans could not be used; a much simpler and smaller building had to suffice.

183. Night view of Art Annex

ART ANNEX (Figs. 183, 184) Until 1948 classes in art, reinstated in 1934, were taught in Presser Hall and in the basement boiler room of the theater. Now a fine workshop was provided in the Art Annex, designed by college architects Barney and Banwell in consultation with Professor John Ballator. Although architecturally unpretentious, it provided many community services and long drew admiring comments from art educators in other institutions. Notable were its inclusion of the first exhibition gallery in the Roanoke area, the Carnegie art library,

184. Old basement studio

and the practice stage for drama and dance. The three-day program for the opening in October 1948 included lectures by curator W. G. Constable of Boston's Museum of Fine Arts, an exhibition of contemporary American paintings, and a formal banquet for the many invited guests.

Notable visitors who came during the 1940s to lecture and exhibit included Josef Albers, Sigfried Giedion, Lamar Dodd, George Rickey, and many others. The new gallery also offered frequent exhibits of the work of local and state artists.

Additional third-floor studios and classroom, designed by Roanoke architects Wells and Meagher, were added in 1954.

185. Nativity miniature from a book of hours

THE MCVITTY RARE BOOK COLLECTION (Figs. 185, 186) Lucy Winton McVitty, member of the board of trustees from 1926 until her death in 1941, is fittingly commemorated at Hollins in the superb collection of manuscripts, incunabula, and rare books given to the college in 1943 by her husband, Samuel Herbert McVitty. Her portrait now hangs in the McVitty Rare Book Room in the Fishburn Library.

The collection of some seventy volumes includes several manuscripts, among them a beautifully illuminated French book of hours, a Franciscan breviary, and an Italian antiphonal. But more notable is the wide range of incunabula. Included are a first edition of the *Nuremberg Chronicle,* the *Vita Christi* of Ludolph of Saxony, a 1491 edition of Dante's *Divine Comedy,* and many other books, plus about

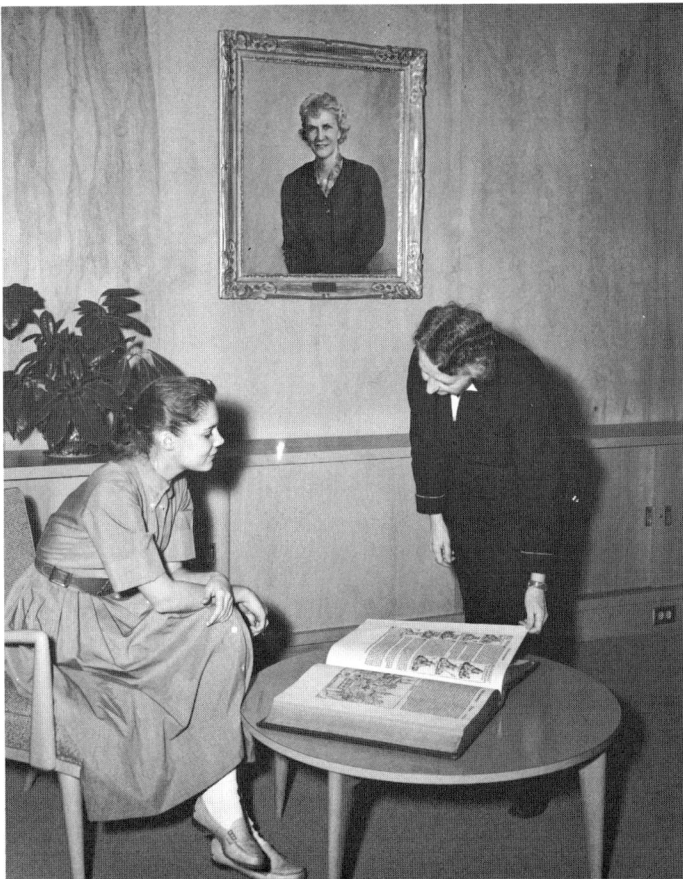

186. Librarian Dorothy Doerr displays the *Nuremberg Chronicle* beneath a portrait of Mrs. McVitty

three hundred leaves from the great early presses of Europe. There are also an early sixteenth-century *Kalendar of Shepherdes* and second and fourth Shakespeare folios. Many books on the history of printing enrich the collection as do titles from distinguished modern presses, such as the famous edition of the *Works of Chaucer* from the Kelmscott Press of William Morris.

187. Honor court, 1949

STUDENT GOVERNMENT (Fig. 187) Student government members, proud of their long-established honor system, increasingly assumed responsibility. In 1933–34 the association had two branches, executive and legislative. A judicial board was added in 1940; it was subdivided into an elected, higher honor court and a lower house board that handled chiefly minor infractions of dormitory rules. The official statement about the honor court's duties, used through the late 1940s, gives some idea of the complex problem of judging one's peers. It read as follows: "Honor Court tries all major offenses, including those involving academic rules, drinking, smoking, places of recreation, driving, dean's slips, overnight absences, rules while in Charlottesville, Lexington, and Blacksburg, late returns from 12:00 and 1:00 special permissions, misuse of cuts for Sunday Chapel and Convocations, and cases referred to it by House Board. Honor Court reserves the right to intervene in cases of unbecoming conduct on the part of any student even when no specific regulation is broken."

188. Freya, 1948

189. Social committee, 1949

STUDENT ORGANIZATIONS (Figs. 188, 189) Pictorial evidence in the *Spinster*s justifies the constant comments in campus newspapers about the overpowering extracurricular activities. Yet purely social clubs were gone: the perennial Cotillion and A.D.A. alone persisted. Most clubs now followed departmental lines.

There were athletic, dramatic, music, international relations, and riding clubs, and from the 1940s on others for philosophy and camera enthusiasts. Subdivisions of these interests included the staffs of the *Spinster,* the newspaper *Student Life* (from 1940 on, *Hollins Columns*), the literary *Cargoes;* Orchesis for modern dance; the Chapel Choir and the intermittent Ensemble. Among honorary societies were Freya, Ye Merrie Masquers, La Chiave (music), the Curie Chemical Society, the Writer's Club, and the Monogram Club (athletics). Added to these were the war and postwar committees, the handbook, the curriculum, and the student service committees (which handled three annual drives—World Student Service, Red Cross, and Save the Children). Then there were the group leaders for freshman orientation, the student marshals, appointed by President Randolph as official hostesses and ushers, the Turner Hall committee, and the social committee. This last took care of Keller, providing cards and ashtrays and frequent changes of nickelodeon records, and in 1946 took charge of Tinker Day.

190. Sophomore prom, 1941

191. Cotillion in gymnasium, 1945

DANCES (Figs. 190, 191) Cotillion members, dressed in slacks and shirts, maintained an old tradition by squiring dates to informal hops in Keller. But true highlights of the college social year were the formal proms, and long hours were spent in glamorizing the gymnasium.

192. Professor Kathleen Jackson with students at Mercy House

193. YWCA Christmas party

YWCA (Figs. 192, 193) *Out on a Limb about College?*—written by students in 1949 for applicants to Hollins—explained: "In the Y.W.C.A. the girls get down to immediate social problems. 'Y' members may be found taking lunch to the Negro school about half a mile from the campus, giving parties for the wide-eyed, lovable children; or you'll find them visiting Mercy House, Roanoke's convalescent home, or cheering up the men at the Veteran's Facility." Mercy House (now McVitty House) was a special project for Hollins girls from the time of its establishment in 1934. Under the guidance of Louise Maddrey and Kathleen Jackson, they took charge of the children's room, dedicated in 1937 to Leila Turner Rath, one of the founders of Mercy House. At Hollins the Y continued its worship and study programs, presented the White Gift service, and in 1940 began to have students conduct chapel services during the week.

ATHLETICS (Figs. 194–197) Pictures of athletes outweighed even the May Day and beauty sections of the *Spinsters* during these years, for at Hollins, as elsewhere, the sports program was extensive, and riding was by now inseparable from the college. Until students were granted the long-sought Thanksgiving vacation in 1950, the annual Odd-Even hockey game remained a major event.

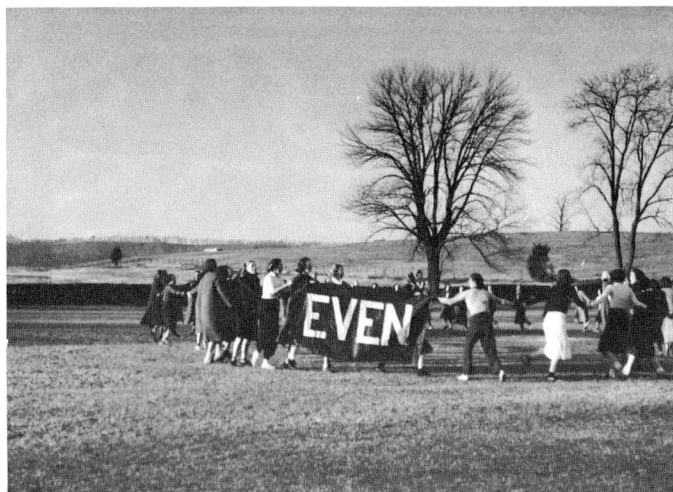

194. Annual hockey game

195. Trail riding

196. Gymkhana: musical chairs, 1946
197. Tennis, 1945
198. *Work Rhythms,* 1935

MODERN DANCE (Figs. 198, 199) Interest was growing in modern dance, which was still under the aegis of the physical education department. The first of the Orchesis dance recitals, *Work Rhythms,* was given in 1935, and in December 1944 Orchesis collaborated with the swimming club to present the first water ballet.

Famous dancers who came to perform ranged from Ruth St. Denis in 1934 to Martha Graham in 1950. Critic John Martin followed the Humphrey-Weidman-Limon Company in 1938.

199. Orchesis, 1945

200. *Death Takes a Holiday,* 1947

201. Scenery production

DRAMATICS (Figs. 200, 201) "Plays of the modern era with real men add up applause for the dramatic association," reported the *Alumnae Quarterly* in the fall of 1939. But girls were still frequently playing men's roles, right up to 1950. They were also creating elaborate scenery and costumes for the fall, spring, and commencement plays that were by now traditional. In 1945 drama and music departments collaborated in a memorable production of *The Pirates of Penzance*.

Many other performers appeared on the Little Theatre stage: the Clare Tree Major's Children's Theatre, the Chekhov and the Barter Players; and summering there were Francis Ballard's Patchwork Players. Among many famous speakers who came were Anton Lang in 1935 to lecture on the Oberammergau Passion Play and John Mason Brown in 1941 to review the Broadway scene.

STUNTS AND FOLLIES (Fig. 202) There were Tinker Day skits and A.D.A. stunts and various frolics throughout the year, but the most ambitious production was that of Senior Stunts, which followed the Halloween masquerade party in the dining hall. Enthusiastic as the audience was for this annual event, nothing matched the wild glee that greeted performers in the quadrennial Faculty Follies. Often these returned the compliment of Senior take-offs of their mentors, but then again the Follies might offer a segment of other experience, as it did in the "Gay Nineties" of 1941 or the "Tobacco Alley" of 1946.

A.D.A. (Fig. 203) "The A.D.A.'s are about as indefinable as the motives of the Marx brothers," said *inside hollins*. Periodically they went into a huddle from which they emerged to shout for new members, who might share their zealously guarded privilege of wearing purple on Tuesdays and take part in their witty or witless performances.

TINKER DAY (Figs. 204–207) From 1940 on incoming freshmen received a sprightly pamphlet written by two seniors and entitled *inside hollins*. This offers a mine of information about the mores of the time. "Climbing Tinker Mountain," freshmen were advised, "is always done in shorts or painter's-farmer's-working-man's overalls." President Randolph wore her white felt hat. Miss Chevraux wore the multi-striped sweater knitted for her by sixteen girls in 1939 (when she retired in 1970 Dean Wheeler inherited it). And Mr. Estes always announced the day.

204.   Mr. Estes announces the Day

205. Starting the climb

206. Riding up the trail to Tinker

207. President Randolph watches A.D.A. stunt

208.   Founder's Day, 1935

FOUNDER'S DAY (Fig. 208) The Hollins weekly *Student Life* reported in 1935 that ceremonies for Founder's Day were to be simplified; no longer would it be an all-day affair. There was always a convocation—with visiting deans, presidents, or chancellors as speakers—and then the senior procession to the cemetery. At night, seniors serenaded the darkened campus from the library steps, often holding glowing lanterns that marked the pattern of the letter *H*.

MAY DAY (Fig. 209) May Day remained one of the most traditional of events through these decades. As in earlier years, there was a charmingly gowned court of lovely girls, music and dancing, and either an original play or a revived classic. Traditionally, also, the new *Spinster*s appeared on May Day, to be distributed on front quad.

209.   May Court, 1940

210. Class Night, 1946
211. Class numerals on the lawn, 1946

CLASS NIGHT (Figs. 210, 211) Class Day by now had become Class Night, with seniors in pastel gowns presented one by one to an admiring audience of parents and friends. Sophomores still made and bore a daisy chain, with which seniors formed their class numerals on the lawn.

VII. Hollins Changes Its Image

The Everett Decade, 1950–1961

MANY faculty members, eyeing and discussing the presidential candidates who visited the campus, dismissed one as too young. But the board of trustees saw in John Rutherford Everett a man experienced in educational matters, full of vigor and ideas, and, like their predecessors of a century before, decided to put their trust in youth. Jack Everett, aged thirty-one when he arrived to take office in July 1950, had within four years acquired four degrees: in 1942 a B.A. from Park College, in 1943 an M.A. from Columbia, in 1944 a B.D. from Union Theological Seminary, and in 1945 a Ph.D. from Columbia. He had taught philosophy, first at Columbia in 1943 and then at Wesleyan from 1945 to 1948, and since 1948 had been chairman of the philosophy department in the School of General Studies at Columbia. He had written numerous articles and two books: *Religion in Economics* and *Religion in Human Experience.* Jack Everett was a man for whom events moved rapidly, and from 1950 on they were to do so for Hollins.

The new president inherited an experienced board of trustees, half of whom had served the college for a decade or longer. New members, added to the nucleus of those who stayed through Dr. Everett's tenure, produced a board of impressive efficiency. It included eminently successful bankers, attorneys, educators, a federal district judge, executives of railway, insurance, newspaper, automotive, oil, and textile corporations, civic leaders, and concerned and capable alumnae. They were working trustees, also, and having chosen a man of action they saw the action begun and much of it carried to completion.

Closely associated with Dr. Everett throughout his tenure was Willard N. James, secretary to the board and vice-president of the college. The two men, colleagues and close friends, made an effective team, complementing and balancing each other. Bill James had his own administrative year when he became acting president after Jack Everett's resignation in 1960. He is included in this chapter, however, partly because his term brought the culmination of projects begun earlier, but chiefly because he was indispensable to the progress of the Everett decade.

Indispensable also was Dean Mary Phlegar Smith, who enthusiastically joined in the formulating of new academic and social programs. While Bill James was taking care of financial matters, new construction, and communication with alumnae and public, Mary Phlegar Smith was inaugurating educational changes and serving particularly well as liaison officer between president and faculty or student body. Working closely with her were the division chairmen. Professors MacDonald, Patterson, and Talmadge continued in these posts throughout the decade, and Professor Wilson served until her retirement in 1958, when Professor Crosby became chairman of Division I.

The new president inherited also an experienced faculty, with some members ready for change, others who were apprehensive or skeptical. Eleven of the thirty-nine faculty members had begun teaching under Miss Matty Cocke; half of the group had arrived at Hollins before or during the war years. Many were wary, not so much of new ideas, as of the danger of insolvency for the college, because they had for so long followed a restricted and conservative path.

But Jack Everett won over many of them at the opening faculty meeting, with a combination of promised benefits and the suggestion that all share in the working out of a new pattern. He proposed that a faculty constitution be drawn up, and that members of committees be elected rather than appointed. Most teachers were delighted to have the chance to define their rights and privileges, and within a year the faculty had established a basic framework that has persisted to the present. Particularly appreciated were two new committees for communication and rapport: one of three members serving as advisory to the president, the other of four members for conference with the trustees. (A year later, faculty were so involved in administration that a committee on committees had to be formed; there was jesting over this but the committee was a useful one.)

Almost at once the new president brought another benefit

to his faculty. He won the approval of the trustees for the creation of a travel and research fund of $3,000 available annually for his scholar-teachers—a fund which would enable them to travel more widely to professional meetings, to undertake research, to publish, perform, compose, paint. A faculty committee was formed to administer this fund, which by 1960 had increased to $10,000. The commitment of Hollins to the scholar-teacher concept was one of the most influential factors in changing the public image of the college and in strengthening it internally. By the late 1950s Hollins faculty members were profiting from the larger grants then available from outside sources. In 1957, for example, the National Science Foundation gave Professor Bolles $20,000 for a study of hunger and thirst motivation in animals, and in 1959 Professor Woods received $18,000 from the National Institute of Mental Health to analyze the effects of early experience on animal behavior. Then in 1960 forty-five beagle pups appeared on campus because Professor Calvin had been granted $24,450 by the U.S. Department of Health, Education, and Welfare for a two-year study of the effect of discipline on the infant dog. Faculty were by now also traveling further afield: in 1957 Professor Montgomery attended the international physics conference in Padua. And faculty dispersed to Honolulu, Ireland, Hyderabad, Salzburg, and elsewhere after the 1959 grant of $10,000 for summer study was made by the Danforth Foundation.

Jack Everett also proposed at his first board meeting that Hollins establish a system of leaves of absence and a new faculty salary scale. When the latter was finally achieved in the spring of 1956, bolstered in part by a grant of $180,000 from the Ford Foundation in that year and $197,000 more in 1957, it was nationally newsworthy. Typical was the comment in the local *Roanoke World-News* that "the decision is as courageous as it is foresighted." Nationwide studies made in the mid-fifties had shown that while salaries in industry had increased by nearly 50 percent since 1940, faculty salaries had decreased. For several years before 1956

President Everett had been reiterating in his *Hollins Herald* columns the fact of this sorry contrast, and finally the board of trustees made what was truly a pioneering move.

The minimum scale now formulated meant an average increase of 22 percent for faculty salaries. Instructors were to begin at $4,500, and salaries rose by $1,000 for each rank up to $7,500 for full professors. (Even then, with the raises, young faculty were disheartened to hear of the $6,000 offered by the National Security Administration to two Hollins girls graduating as mathematics majors.) By the fall of 1958 an even better range was set. Minimums remained the same, but maximums allowed for flexibility within ranks since they offered, from instructor upward, $6,000, $7,500, $9,000, and $12,000. The Hollins average salary by 1959 was $7,340 against a national average of $6,580. In 1959, also, the appreciated fringe benefits of major medical and group life insurance were arranged for Hollins faculty and staff by James.

President Everett's appointments to the staff were in part replacements, in part additions chosen either to introduce new departments or to strengthen certain areas. As college enrollments expanded—from 329 students in 1950 to 550 in 1955 and to 678 in 1960—naturally so did the size of the faculty. Between 1950 and 1960 the number of full professors increased from 9 to 17 (plus two visiting professors), associates from 9 to 17, assistants from 10 to 23, and instructors from 11 to 14. The lower proportion of instructors illustrates Jack Everett's policy of appointing experienced teachers, or those with perhaps less experience but with advanced degrees. By 1959, 85 percent of the faculty held the Ph.D. or its equivalent.

Faculty appointed by 1955 who were to stay at Hollins included H. Lamar Crosby and M. Barbara Zeldin in philosophy, Jesse Zeldin and John Allen in English, Dean Goodsell and Paula Levine in drama and dance, John Diercks and Oscar McCullough in music, Lewis Thompson in art, Roberta Stewart in chemistry, G. Cary White and John P. Wheeler in sociology and political science, F. Joseph Mc-

Guigan in psychology, and George Gordh to teach religion and to serve as the first resident chaplain Hollins had had since 1933. Harold Arbour began the new program in commercial science. The former single office handling admissions and registrar's activities was divided; Ann Splitstone continued with admissions and Margaret Eldridge was appointed registrar. Faculty who were to move on, but who were influential in building up departments over a period of several years, included Dorothy Montgomery and Richard Garrett in physics, Jesse Thompson in biology, Allen Calvin in psychology, Anita Ernouf and Maurice Sullivan in modern languages, Edmund Wright in music, Stuart Degginger and John Garruto in English, Jack Andrews in drama, and Mary Thompson in physical education.

Joining these between 1956 and 1961 were a number who were to remain at Hollins. In this group were Ralph Steinhardt and Beatrice Gushee in chemistry, Paul Woods in psychology, Lowell Wine in statistics, Claude Thompson in mathematics, John Moore in English, Fernand Marty in French, Marjorie Berkley and Guy Burkholder in physical education, and Alvord Beardslee to teach religion and to assume the office of chaplain in 1959. Alumna Robbie Hunt Burton came as director of alumnae relations and Joseph Milward as director of the new office of development. Again there were individuals who stayed for a number of years, helping to strengthen departments. These included Kermit Hunter in drama, Louis D. Rubin, Jr., in English, Ulysse Desportes in art, Walter Hanchett and Robert Ramsey in history, Thomas Hanna in philosophy and religion, Robert Bolles in psychology, and Alexander Vasiliev in Russian.

Staff members with long-term service included Roy Obenchain, who assumed the responsible post of steward in 1951 and in 1957 became assistant to superintendent of buildings and grounds John T. Griffin. Then there were supervisors of buildings Mildred Durbin and Mary Jo Whitman, steward Jack B. Woodson, laundry manager Gordon Obenchain, head nurse Fay Ellen McCollum, and many others. In addition to all these, there were the visiting scholars whom President Everett brought to Hollins for a semester or longer, and the lecturers who came for shorter periods.

At that first board meeting in 1950, chairman C. Francis Cocke reaffirmed the faith of the trustees in the "earnest and felt need for women with a liberal arts education." He added that such an education implied two great objectives, and these objectives, in his words, appeared in Hollins catalogues from 1952 on. They read:

1. The liberation of the mind and spirit from unconsciously and uncritically accepted values and propositions, to develop qualities of wisdom, virtue, and civility.

2. The establishment of a firm foundation of fact and theory which will serve as a frame of reference and a guide for adequately meeting the new problems and situations which are bound to arise in the future lives of our students.

Cocke concluded with a paragraph from which another sentence was frequently quoted: "To seek the truth and to discover the abiding and eternal values is man's most meaningful quest."

In order better to implement these aims, the president and board asked the faculty to study and to rework the curriculum. What seemed at times like endless discussion led finally to the inauguration of the New Curriculum two years later. This scheme, keyed to the assumed maturity of the students, was in 1952 distinctly progressive, both for Hollins and for education in general. Some years earlier Dean Mary Phlegar Smith had urged that Hollins follow the lead of the larger universities in adopting what was then termed General Education. In a 1946 article for the *Alumnae Quarterly* she had explained the idea of integrated courses, mentioning Harvard's Great Texts of Literature and Columbia's Great Books, Harvard's Western Thought and Institutions and Columbia's Contemporary Civilization. Finally, in 1952, she had her Hollins parallels to these.

The Hollins New Curriculum included two required general education courses for freshmen. One was Humanities, subtitled by chairman Mary Vincent Long "The Drama of Man," for it was planned as an "introduction to some of the persistent human problems men have explored in philosophical, religious, and literary studies of man as man." Freshmen began the first semester's work, for example, with Arthur Miller's *Death of a Salesman* and ended it with T. S. Eliot's *Murder in the Cathedral,* reading selections from the Greeks, the Bible, Saint Augustine's *Confessions,* and *The Divine Comedy* in between. The second prescribed course was entitled "Characteristic Institutions of American Society." G. Cary White, its chairman, pronounced its theme: "What then is this American, this new man?" Not only institutions but historical roots, ideas, and contemporary issues were studied under the guidance of the social science faculty. The multiple sections in both courses were limited to twenty students to encourage both discussion and writing.

Required also for a Hollins degree were year courses in a laboratory science and in art, music, or drama, two years of physical education, and the passing of an exit examination in a foreign language. Except for the freshman courses, requirements might be met in any year, including the senior one. "We have repudiated the splitting of the program into an upper college and a lower college," wrote Dean Smith for the *Hollins Herald,* "because we are convinced of the essential integrity of a four-year liberal arts program." The criterion of flexibility led also to the abandonment of many former prerequisites and to the creation of many semester courses in lieu of full year sequences.

In addition to the core courses, there was still specialization in a major field, and a greater variety of possible majors came into being. Subjects formerly paired were now divorced, such as mathematics from physics, and religion from philosophy. Separate majors were offered in economics, sociology, and politics (political science renamed), and newly offered in 1952 were drama and a divisional major in science. Statistics, which in 1958 had been separated from economics-sociology and joined to mathematics, offered in 1959 what was probably the first major in a woman's college. Many departments were reinstated, as was German, or

augmented, as was drama by dance. Notably new was a program in Russian studies. Professor Hanchett, writing for the *Alumnae Bulletin* in 1960, reported that a 1959 study had found "a perfect vacuum of knowledge about the Soviet Union existing in many schools." But Professors Hanchett and Jesse and Barbara Zeldin, all experts on Russia, had already in the spring of 1958 decided to inaugurate a Russian studies program, and this was done in 1959. The following year, when Professor Alexander Nicholas Vasiliev, formerly of Yale, arrived to conduct the language courses, about a hundred students were enrolled in the various aspects of the program.

The New Curriculum also initiated a number of career-oriented courses, because the policy of general education included the acquisition of skills. Among these were secretarial training, student teaching in the local schools, and certain physical education courses: life saving, recreational leadership, and water safety. All gave college credits but were limited to junior and senior elections. An office for vocational guidance was also established in 1952.

The carefully planned and implemented requirements of the New Curriculum were not, upon trial, wholly successful. Many students and faculty members were particularly unhappy with the language exit examination, and it was made optional after 1957, so that some students might again exit through course work. American Society was dropped in 1958 and replaced by two courses, one in European history and the other chosen from economics, sociology, politics, or psychology.

A semester afield in the School of Social Sciences and Public Affairs of American University was made available in 1951, when Hollins joined a group of twenty colleges cooperating in a Washington Semester program. Then in 1954 came the exciting news of Hollins's own year of foreign study and travel: Hollins Abroad, with the fanfare of the send-off for the first group headed for Paris on the S.S. *Liberté.*

Among incentives to serious study that opened up in the

1950s, perhaps most notable were the increasing opportunities for undergraduates to pursue research. Science departments led in this activity. In April 1956, for example, three sophomores read papers before the five hundred psychologists—and no other undergraduates—gathered in Atlanta for a regional meeting, and a few years later chemistry students began going to the national laboratories in Oak Ridge, Tennessee, and Brookhaven, Long Island, to do experimental work. In 1959 the National Science Foundation gave Hollins a grant of $5,700 to pay undergraduates engaged in research in varied fields.

Both faculty and students had long been aware that outstanding scholars should be recognized, and an honor society named Pi Epsilon Mu was organized in 1950–51 by faculty members of Phi Beta Kappa and Sigma Xi. By 1959 Hollins had received its own chapter of Psi Chi, the honorary society for psychology, and then in 1960 a club of Sigma Xi, honoring scientific research. Finally, the merit of another application for a Phi Beta Kappa chapter was recognized, and one was granted in the fall of 1961. The growing concern of students for scholarship was reflected in the considerable space *Hollins Columns* gave to news of graduate study grants; from 1954 on, for example, Hollins girls annually won Fulbright grants for foreign study.

The decision to follow the pattern of industry and shift to a five-day week for classes came in 1956, and along with this pleasant change, all students were given the privilege of regulating their class attendance. There were still no-cut days before and after holidays, but these were finally reduced to twenty-four hours, rather than forty-eight.

The practice of making multiple applications to colleges spread rapidly in the 1950s, creating difficulties for admission offices over the country. Hollins tuition fees were also steadily rising: to $1,500 in 1953, $2,100 in 1956, $2,300 in 1961. More scholarships were now made available to Hollins applicants, including newly offered ones for freshmen and foreign students. As further inducements, there were options for early admission, advanced placement, and the taking of the language exit examination upon arrival at Hollins. A new system of freshman orientation and advising was inaugurated, with some twenty faculty members replacing the former single freshman adviser. Persistence to graduation was still to fluctuate from year to year, but the 75 percent graduating in 1959 indicated a significant improvement over the 50 percent of 1955. The number of girls from southern states dropped markedly during the decade, from 71 to 56 percent.

A new committee on development was formed in 1952, headed by R. H. Smith and including Mrs. Alfred I. duPont, Mrs. George Scott Shackelford, Paul Buford, and LeRoy H. Smith. A major building fund campaign was also launched, directed by R. H. Smith and Mrs. R. Finley Gayle, national alumnae chairman. Joseph U. Milward came to the campus in 1956 to head a new development office, and an annual giving campaign was instituted, supported by scores of alumnae. President Everett had also persuaded his board to borrow some $650,000, an unprecedented indebtedness for Hollins. The decade, then, was marked by great financial change. The total annual budget expanded from $648,000 in 1950 to $1,714,000 in 1960, and the endowment rose from about $400,000 to a market value of over $3 million, primarily through the great generosity of Mrs. duPont. Most helpful also, however, was a $20,000 grant received from the U.S. Steel Foundation under its Aid to Education program. The value of the physical plant rose concurrently, from $1.5 million to about $4.5 million, for during the decade there was literally continuous building and the campus was extended in all directions.

By fall of 1951, five faculty houses had been built on the slopes of the old cow pasture, upper floors of the Susanna Infirmary had been converted into dormitories, part of Botetourt Hall's porch had been enclosed to provide a faculty dining area, and new cafeteria equipment had been installed. Tinker Tea House became a dormitory in 1952. In 1953 the new Turner Hall was ready, and the process of placing all utility wires underground was begun. In 1954 a third story was added to the Art Annex, the power house and other utilities were modernized, and automatic sprinklers for fire prevention were installed in all the old dormitories. When the Fishburn Library and the Randolph Hall dormitory were ready for use in 1955, the Cocke Library had been completely rebuilt for administrative and business offices, a larger bookstore and post office had been created in Botetourt basement, and the Tea House had undergone another conversion, now becoming an infirmary. In 1956 riding rings and stables were built. In 1957 an anonymous donor provided a small greenhouse with an animal laboratory for psychology, and the new chapel was begun. By 1958 not only was the chapel completed but there were more faculty houses and apartments, with two more to rise in 1959, and Bradley Chapel was converted into a small auditorium. Broad concrete walks appeared around the front quadrangle, which was now closed to general traffic. Outer parking lots and new roads had already been constructed. The Keller in the basement of Main Building was converted into offices during the summer of 1959, and in 1960 Encyclopedia Britannica Films erected the Hill Building behind the old parsonage.

Among the many issues that stirred the campus and beset the student government during this decade, most discussed was the question of the viability of the honor system. "Honor or System?" This headline for an editorial in *Hollins Columns* gave the gist of the matter. One point of view held that "the honor system is a way of life and in everything we do we are honor bound." The other held that system was antithetic to honor, which was personal. The chairman of the house board stated in 1957 that "many of the rules we agree to live by have little relation to ethical codes, honor, or moral values. Many are technicalities that facilitate group living." In 1957, then, jurisdiction of the honor court was specifically limited to "breaches of academic honesty, lying, stealing, and serious social violations." All other infractions of rules were handled by the house board. Argument was continuing, however, in 1960–61, for many students felt that the honor court should not deal with social violations, however serious they might be. Double reporting had been voted out in 1951–52, but students were still ex-

pected to assume responsibility for misconduct by others. Obviously a fairly strong statement about this matter was necessary some years later, for the *Handbook* of 1959 said: "As a member of the college community, a student is obligated to call misconduct to the attention of the offender and see that she reports herself, and MUST feel a personal responsibility to do so in cases where life, property, or reputation of the college is endangered."

Another major issue was that of compulsion. An editorial in *Hollins Columns* of March 20, 1958, stated firmly: "We no longer want to be *made* anything—cultured, civic, or Christian. We want the *opportunity to become*—to become of our own choosing that which we wish to be. We appreciate and welcome guidance, but we wholeheartedly deplore any kind of requirement which interferes with our own rights as maturing individuals."

By 1958 a good many rights had been obtained. Since 1952 seniors had been permitted to have their own two-toned or convertible cars. Specific permission for commercial passenger flights was not required from 1955 on (it was about time, for a Hollins junior was Piedmont Airline's millionth passenger in 1954). All curfew rules for Lexington, Charlottesville, and Blacksburg were annulled in 1956. But, although students might now regulate their own class attendance, there were still only limited cuts available for chapel and for convocations. Ironically, the protest against required chapel reached a peak just as the duPont Chapel was being completed—a logical timing, nevertheless, for compulsory chapel had by then been dropped by practically every other college, as Chaplain Alvord Beardslee informed the conservative alumnae. "Large numbers of students," said an editorial in the *Columns* in 1958, "no longer feel that they can reconcile religious services with freedom of religion or of conscience. . . . The students do not want to desecrate that new place of worship by forced attendance." Then there was the matter of required convocations, long protested. The administration promised in the spring of 1959 to make a statement about this by the fall, but when it came it was somewhat equivocal. "A convocation," said the ruling, "is a program which a student is required to attend." Henceforth certain programs were labeled convocations, and a given number of students could absent themselves by signing a sheet posted on the bulletin board.

Yet another issue of the decade is defined by a new category that appeared in the *Handbooks* in 1953, headed "Standards of Dress" and aimed rather futilely at keeping students in skirts. Compared to the few sentences in earlier handbooks about not loitering in pants, the standards were now detailed and lengthy and incited expression of opinions in the campus newspaper. An editorial of October 1954 lamented: "Now they are down to short sleeves, shorter shorts, and no shoes at all!" And the campus activities committee set up an extracurricular course in good grooming, run by Smartwear-Irving Saks. But many students chose to misinterpret the advice given them by alumnae admissions representatives (coached by the Splitstone-Henn manual of 1950, *Hand in Hand*): "This is a country college and dress is simple and casual."

There was much debate, also, about what was known as the hotel-motel rule, effective in September 1953. Hollins girls were forbidden to enter hotel or motel rooms with dates, and serious problems arose because parties in those rooms were increasingly commonplace and popular. Finally the ruling was modified for 1960–61, but "ONLY WHEN CHAPERONED."

Along with the undergraduates on campus at the opening of college in September 1958, there appeared three male students, pioneer candidates for the new M.A. being offered by the department of psychology. They received their degrees in 1959, in which year an M.A. was also offered in linguistics. Then in 1960 the department of English offered an M.A. program encompassing creative writing, literary criticism, and contemporary literature. This program, under the direction of Professor Rubin, called for the appointment of an annual writer-in-residence, and American critic and novelist John W. Aldridge was invited to Hollins for the spring term of 1961. All M.A. programs were open to both men and women, but the majority of candidates in the early years were in fact male. The linguistics offering was soon dropped, but both English and psychology graduate programs were to flourish.

As in earlier decades, the campus was utilized by various groups during the summer months. A Hollins day camp was run for several years by Professor Grace Chevraux, a science course was given in 1952 for student nurses from the Roanoke Memorial Hospital, and in 1960 began a week-long music camp for the Roanoke Youth Symphony. Hollins also administered, in 1959 and 1960, one of the dozen language institutes for high-school teachers established under the National Defense Education Act; Hollins was the only small college chosen for this educational service.

By 1960 Hollins, old as it was, gave evidence of a capacity for growth matching that of much younger colleges; it exhibited, in fact, a remarkable youthful vigor. As Dean Smith reported to the alumnae, Hollins had won "widespread recognition and increasing academic stature," and physically it had greatly changed. But its youthful president resigned that spring. He was to embark in September on the chancellorship of the Municipal College System of the City of New York, with seven colleges and some 90,000 students under his jurisdiction. Bill James was persuaded to serve as acting president until a new administrator could take charge, and the search for Hollins's fifth president began.

investigating the right of free men to participate in all educational and cultural pursuits. He lectured, preached, was active in a variety of enterprises—notably in the establishment and support of the Virginia Foundation of Independent Colleges. But his energy was given chiefly to Hollins, where he wholeheartedly participated in everything from the planning of policy to clowning in faculty follies.

PRESIDENT JOHN R. EVERETT (Fig. 212) When Jack Everett relinquished his post at Hollins, an editorial in the *Columns* stated that "the students feel fortunate and proud to have had a share in his educational career . . . he has gained the respect and admiration of the campus not only as an educator, but also as a truly dynamic leader and teacher and as a friend." Many faculty and alumnae agreed. He had maintained at Hollins an open-door policy, and, even with a larger faculty, Jack Everett knew each individual as well as his predecessors had known their colleagues. During his first year as president, he had visited every alumnae club, and he continued to keep in close touch with alumnae workers. Students on campus found him willing to listen and to support them, and Hollins Abroaders delighted in his Paris parties.

Responsibilities and honors outside the college came to him from the first year, when the U.S. Junior Chamber of Commerce chose him as one of the ten outstanding young men in the country, and the second, when he represented the United States on a UNESCO committee

WILLARD N. JAMES (Fig. 214) Hollins could not have had a better acting president than Willard N. James for the interim year of 1960–61. On his appointment, board president C. Francis Cocke remarked, "Mr. James is thoroughly familiar with every detail of the operation of the college, and his leadership will insure that there will be no interruption in the progress of Hollins." Bill James, native of Irvington, Lancaster County, Virginia, graduate of the College of William and Mary, manager of the News and Publications Bureau at Carnegie Institute of Technology, had in fact been brought to Hollins in 1940 to further expansion and progress. Now, after the frustrations of the war years, during which he assumed the difficult role of business manager, his abilities were properly utilized.

From 1948 on, he took charge of the Hollins public relations program, initiating in 1950 the invaluable *Hollins Herald,* which he edited until 1958. In 1952 he was promoted to the post of vice-president and treasurer, overseeing the myriad details of business and building operations with acumen and equanimity. His special forte for public relations was shown also in his active participation in varied concerns of the Roanoke community, such as the Symphony Society, the Community Hospital, and the Chamber of Commerce.

Bill James shared other talents with his colleagues: his wit as raconteur, his expertise in tennis and sailing, his love of music. As charter member of the Hollins Hambones, he shared with a delighted audience his skill on the banjo.

EVERETT INAUGURAL (Fig. 213) The installation of John Rutherford Everett as fourth head of Hollins was held on April 15–16, 1951. His father Monroe G. Everett, president of Trinity University in San Antonio, presided over the first evening service, at which the Reverend James A. Pike, Chaplain of Columbia, delivered the inaugural sermon.

At the next morning's ceremonies, C. Francis Cocke formally gave Dr. Everett his charge. The new president immediately won his student audience by proclaiming the next day a holiday, and then gave his inaugural address, "Freedom and Tradition." He mentioned the need for "lively concern for new ideas, criticism, and experimentation" but reminded his listeners that "knowledge of past experience and past development is the substance and content of education." "We must never forget," he said, "that our educational institutions are the seekers, not the purveyors, of truth." Ordway Tead, chairman of the Board of Higher Education of the City of New York, followed with a talk entitled "Higher Education as a Public Trust."

The ceremonies were attended by representatives from 142 colleges and universities and from 35 learned societies and educational institutions, to whom Hollins extended its traditional hospitality.

BOARD OF TRUSTEES, 1951 (Fig. 215) All members of the board attended the inaugural ceremonies and posed with the new president. Appearing in the front row, from left to right, are Judge Alfred D. Barksdale, Board President C. Francis Cocke, Dr. Everett, Mrs. Charles P. Orr, and LeRoy H. Smith. In the center are Mrs. Alfred I. duPont, Mrs. Leonard Muse, Miss Orlie Pell, Paul C. Buford, L. J. Boxley, and Frank W. Rogers. In the back row are Mrs. Jason B. Sowell, Mrs. R. Finley Gayle, Jr., Mrs. Barton W. Morris, Mrs. Milton R. Morgan, Junius P. Fishburn, and R. H. Smith, vice-president of the board.

BOARD OF TRUSTEES, 1957 (Fig. 216) These trustees were photographed at their meeting in October 1957 in the new board room of the Fishburn Library. Present were, from the left, Mrs. A. C. Dick, Paul C. Buford, Lewis F. Powell, Jr., Mrs. George Scott Shackelford, Jr., Mrs. Barton W. Morris, English Showalter, Stuart T. Saunders, Dr. Francis P. Gaines, Mrs. P. R. Gilmer, R. H. Smith, Frank W. Rogers, J. Harvie Wilkinson, Jr., Mrs. William C. Styron, Board Secretary Willard N. James, C. Francis Cocke, President Everett, and Mrs. Alfred I. duPont.

Other trustees of the Everett decade included Cyrus R. Osborn, elected in 1956, Stewart P. Coleman, elected in 1958, and alumnae members Miss Mary Monroe Penick, Mrs. Harry C. Stuart, Mrs. Charles R. Younts, and Miss Susanna P. Turner.

MRS. ALFRED I. DUPONT (Fig. 217) At the close of the dedication service for the new chapel, President Everett awarded Mrs. Alfred I. duPont the first honorary degree ever given by Hollins, naming her a Doctor of Humane Letters. "The many and varied good works of this gracious lady are known to but a few," he said. "Her concern to improve educational opportunities, her compassion for suffering children, her interest in the arts, and her dedication to the preservation of the finest in our country's tradition all mark her as an outstanding person. Beyond these things, this fair daughter of Virginia embodies the nobility of character, the refinement of manner, and the depth of understanding which signify a true and responsible citizen of Christian civilization."

Jessie Ball duPont—herself a teacher, a sound businesswoman, an administrator in fields ranging from wartime Red Cross work to college trusteeships—found time to share amply with Hollins her wisdom and her charm. So generous was her financial aid that members of the Hollins family began to call her their second founder. And they also loved her. Introduced to Mrs. duPont when she arrived for her first board of trustees meeting in 1944, faculty were amazed that she could identify each by name and department; they shared from the beginning in her continuous warm personal commitment to Hollins and rejoiced in her graciousness as much as in her beneficence.

OPENING FACULTY MEETINGS (Fig. 218) To further communication, President Everett replaced opening faculty meetings by weekends devoted to college business and getting-acquainted parties. Old and new faculty met at Hot Springs, at Natural Bridge, and then at nearby Loch Haven. The group picture shows the faculty gathered at Natural Bridge in 1953.

VISITING PROFESSORS (Fig. 219) President Everett early inaugurated a program that brought visiting scholars to the campus for a semester or longer. First of these, in 1951–52, was Lauder Visiting Professor of Philosophy Francis C. Becker. In following years came such eminent figures as James Southall Wilson in English, Clair Francis Littell in history and political science, French author Jacques Lusseyran, economist Albion G. Taylor, and psychologist Charles Hanley.

Most colorful of all visitors was Dr. Enid Starkie, who came for the fall semester of 1959. Reader in French Literature and Fellow of Somerville College at Oxford, member of the Irish Academy of Letters, Commander of the Order of the British Empire, and internationally renowned author of a score of critical studies on Baudelaire, Rimbaud, and other writers, Miss Starkie not only endeared herself to Hollins but was in turn completely charmed by the college. After her untimely death in 1970, Hollins received the impressive bequest of her collection of some 5,000 volumes of French and English literature, her home at Oxford, and other benefactions.

Flanking Miss Starkie in the photograph are Jaroslav Pelikan and Edouard Morot-Sir, her fellow participants at Hollins's centennial celebration honoring Henri Bergson, held in October 1959.

219.   Jaroslav Pelikan, Enid Starkie, and Edouard Morot-Sir

220.   Chester Bowles leads discussion, 1954

221.   Dr. Kirtley Mather

VISITING LECTURERS (Figs. 220, 221) Required all-campus convocations diminished in numbers, and opening convocations and commencements from 1953 on remained family affairs, with talks by President Everett, members of the faculty or board, or visiting professors.

But many guests came to lecture to academic groups, often staying for two days or more. The new humanities program, for instance, brought Moses Hadas, Gertrude Smith, Richard Lattimore, and Mark Van Doren to lecture on the Greeks, Lewis M. Hammond on Dante, and Wilhelm Pauck on the Reformation. The growing interest in Eastern history and culture, stimulated by Professor MacDonald, led to the invitation of experts on India such as artist Mukul Dey, embassy secretary N. B. Menon, and former ambassador Chester Bowles. Mr. and Mrs. William Henderson lectured on Communist China, Joseph J. Zasloff on Indochina, Alan Paton on Africa, Ralph Braibanti on Japan, and Raymond L. Garthoff on Soviet affairs. Science students met nuclear experts such as William Kieffer, James R. Arnold, and Martin Deutsch, and the science seminars established at the end of the decade featured regular visits by Michael Scriven and Kirtley Mather.

MARSHALL LECTURES (Fig. 222) Dr. Charles B. Marshall, member of the Policy Planning Staff of the Department of State, came to Hollins in 1951 to participate in a Founder's Day panel on foreign affairs, together with Congressman A. A. Ribicoff of Connecticut and Edgar A. Mowrer, radio commentator and author. Marshall returned in October 1953 to deliver the Bessie Carter Randolph Lectures on Foreign Policy, which appeared the following year in a well-received book, *The Limits of Foreign Policy.*

President Everett commented that he hoped Marshall's campus lectures would give students who had been "subjected to widespread and violent discussion of the external relations of these United States . . . a sane and firm platform of fact and theory for understanding foreign policy."

NEW FACULTY ROW (Fig. 223) The old cow pasture provided fertile ground for the trees, shrubs, and flowers soon planted by faculty occupants of the houses and small apartments that sprang up like mushrooms in the summers of 1951, '58, '59, and '62. The first five houses were built by B. F. Parrott from stock plans; the later ones were erected by the firm of Maxey Homes. All followed a common design of modified ranch style.

223.   Air view of campus, 1953, showing faculty houses and Turner Hall

156

TURNER HALL (Fig. 224) Despite some strongly voiced objections to flat roofs and stark walls, the new dormitories introduced to the campus a streamlined contemporary style, modest in design and planned for less expensive maintenance than the older buildings demanded.

Mrs. Joseph Turner broke ground for the first dormitory, named as a memorial to her husband and his sister, Leila Turner Rath. Architects W. Pope Barney and Roy W. Banwell chose to echo East Building in the plan, but in lieu of East's balconies there was a snack bar with a terrace opening on the Beale Memorial Garden. Turner, built by contractor B. F. Parrott at a cost of about $320,000, was in use in September 1953.

RANDOLPH HALL (Fig. 225) A second dormitory, named for President Emeritus Bessie Carter Randolph, was ready for occupancy in the fall of 1955. Architects for this $375,000 building were Frantz and Addkison of Roanoke, and the general contractor was J. W. Turner. Housing some eighty-two students in comparison to Turner Hall's sixty-eight, Randolph initiated a move to back campus. It admitted also the need for parking lot and sun deck as well as an outdoor terrace.

HOLLINS ABROAD (Figs. 226, 227) Hollins Abroad, originated during a discussion of Dean Smith with the freshman advisers and developed by President Everett and Professor Stuart Degginger, became one of the most exciting programs of the decade. It differed from other foreign study plans in several ways, notably that it began in the middle of the sophomore year, included a long summer tour, and required no knowledge of French for the residency in Paris.

The core of the early curriculum was the Cours de civilisation française at the Sorbonne, augmented by courses at other institutes of the University of Paris. Hollins girls were lodged with French professional families. The pioneer group of thirty students sailed with Professor Degginger in February 1955 on the S.S. *Liberté* and with him toured fourteen countries of western Europe the following summer.

Until the mid-1960s one or two Hollins faculty members accompanied the students each year, in order to keep close ties with the college. The tours were gradually extended—to Russia with Professors Jesse and Barbara Zeldin in 1958, and in the 1960s as far east as Iran with professional guide George Guisi, who was long associated with Hollins Abroad travel.

MUSICAL PERFORMANCES (Fig. 228) Music, perennially featured at Hollins, brought to Hollins in the fifties, as before, performers too numerous to list. But among others coming during the decade may be mentioned pianists Rosalyn Tureck, Gina Bachauer, Beveridge Webster, Erich Itor Kahn, Grant Johanessen, Iren Marik, Michel Block, and John Browning; violinists Joseph Knitzer, Alfredo Campoli, Robert Gerle; organists Robert Noehren, Philip Gehring, and André Marchal. A memorable event of 1953 was the Salzburg Marionettes' performance of *The Magic Flute*. (For this, the theater overflowed, and henceforth admission tickets were required.) Vocal artists included Lotte Lehmann, John Langstaff, Nell Rankin, Lois Marshall, William DuPree, and alumnae Mary Curtis-Verna and Jane Stuart Smith. Carilloneurs Arthur Bigelow and Wendell Wescott rang the new bells. And notable ensemble groups included the Hungarian String Quartet, the Mozart Orchestra, the Quartetto Italiano, and the Netherlands Chamber Choir.

228.   Lotte Lehmann with music students, 1951

229.   *Dido and Aeneas*, 1957

DANCE AND DRAMA (Fig. 229) Growing interest in modern dance classes, now incorporated with drama, produced enthusiastic audiences and also participants in the master classes now offered by visitors. Among these were José Limon, Charles Weidman, Daniel Nagrin, and the Indian dancer Miss Sita Poovaiah, who spent a week at Hollins.

The Dublin Players, the Canadian Players, and Players, Inc., of Washington, D.C., presented numerous performances. So did Hollins students, who had the chance to participate in the premieres of plays such as Kermit Hunter's *The Paper Rose* or Jesse Zeldin's *Idol of the Tribe*. Particularly popular was the Christmas performance in 1954 of Menotti's *Amahl and the Night Visitors,* and it was repeated the following year.

DAVE GARROWAY SHOW (Fig. 230) Students milled around a campus strewn with cables early on the morning of May 16, 1956, when Dave Garroway's Today Show was televised from Hollins. The V.M.I. Glee Club and the Roanoke Symphony Orchestra joined the Hollins participants; musicians installed on the steps of Cocke Memorial Building practiced from 4:00 A.M. on, and the cafeteria ran all night. Students were happy because this was the last class day of the year. But the greatest rejoicing was that of the faculty and staff, for in the early morning mail appeared unprecedented bonus checks. Mrs. Alfred I. duPont, with a characteristic sympathetic gesture, had given $40,000 to be distributed. Taken all together, it was a memorable day.

231. Fishburn Library

FISHBURN LIBRARY (Figs. 231–235) The new library was dedicated on Founder's Day, 1956, in memory of Junius Parker Fishburn, Roanoke publisher, member of the board of trustees from 1931 to 1954, and generous benefactor to the college. Speakers at the dedication were author Elizabeth Janeway; William R. Parker, executive secretary of the Modern Language Association; and Keyes D. Metcalf, librarian emeritus of Harvard, who had served as consultant in the planning. Major credit for the meticulous consideration of every aspect of the functioning of the library, however, must go to Hollins's own librarian, Dorothy Doerr.

232. Rear view of Fishburn Library

233. Reading area, Fishburn Library

234. Periodical area and terrace

235. Moving the books

Designed in contemporary style by Frantz and Addkison and built by H. A. Lucas and Sons at a cost of $440,000, the library employed modular construction, extensive glass, and primary colors for much of its decor. The asymmetric balance of the facade was accented by a black marble plaque near the entrance doors. It was the first air-conditioned building on the campus and offered further amenities such as smoking alcoves, individual study carrels, and an outdoor terrace. A board room for conferences and an archives collection was named for Rena Rice Geer, and a rare book room for Lucy Winton McVitty.

Superintendent of buildings and grounds John Griffin arranged for the transfer of books from the old to the new library in a way both ingenious and fitting to southwestern Virginia. They were packed in boxes borrowed from local apple orchards, moved by jeep-drawn wagons, and carried on conveyor belts.

236. duPont Chapel, front view

JESSIE BALL DUPONT CHAPEL (Figs. 236–240) The new chapel was the felicitous result of devoted designing by architects Randolph Frantz and William Addkison and professors Arthur Talmadge and George Gordh. It reflected a warm personal concern, from the contributions made by 735 alumnae and 180 other friends to the production of the seal for its facade by art students.

Chosen for its exterior was a modified Colonial style harmonizing with the older campus buildings. But the interior was modern in spirit. Emphasized was the natural quality of materials: slate, greenstone, and marble for the flooring, brick for the walls, pine for the spanning arches, and fir for the ceiling. Vertical lines accented the height of the sanctuary and focused attention on the great cross made by Lewis Armento from one piece of ebony.

More than gratitude for Mrs. duPont's generous gifts to the chapel fund prompted the dedication in her name. As an alumnae group said to the trustees, "Mrs. duPont has become an integral part of Hollins in things of the spirit." Another most generous gift of $100,000 was given by Mr. and Mrs. Toddie L. Wynne (Imogene Avis Young, Hollins '17) of Dallas, in memory of Mrs. Wynne's mother, Allie Nash Young (Hollins '90). This gift provided for the Meditation Chapel, the organs, and the carillon.

The final cost of the whole complex was $715,000. Building was begun by contractors H. A. Lucas and Sons in June 1957, and the first service was held on Sunday evening, September 21, 1958.

164

237. duPont Chapel, side view

238. duPont Chapel, interior

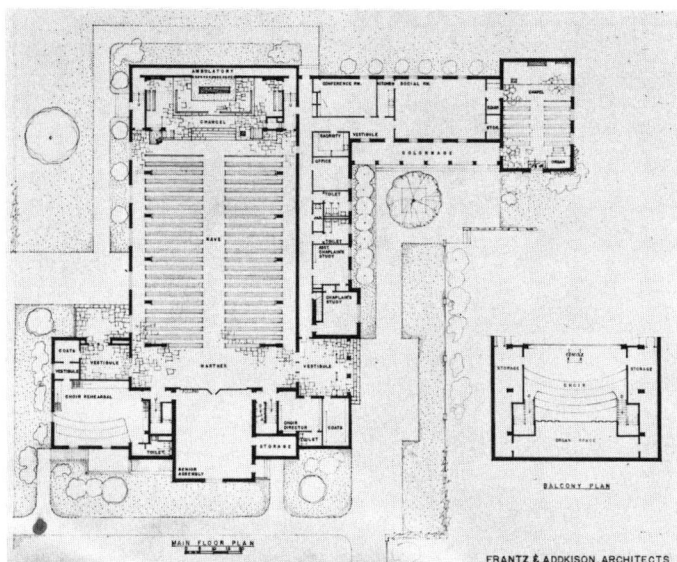

239. duPont Chapel, plan

240. Students complete college seal for chapel gable

duPont Chapel Dedication (Fig. 241) The duPont Chapel was formally presented by Board Chairman C. Francis Cocke to President Everett at the dedication service on February 27, 1959. The Right Reverend Frank A. Juhan, retired Bishop of Florida, gave the invocation, and Chaplain Gordh read the Litany of Dedication. The sermon was delivered by the Reverend John Baillie, Dean of the Divinity Faculty of the University of Edinburgh. The Chapel Choir, augmented by many alumnae members, sang a special anthem, "The Gate of Heaven," composed as a gift for the occasion by Randall Thompson.

As preludes, Kermit Hunter's specially written play, *Homecoming in Magdala,* was performed at the chancel on February 20, and Fenner Douglass of Oberlin College gave an organ recital on February 21. Sculpture and paintings by Pierre Daura, stressing religious themes, were exhibited in the Art Annex Gallery.

The Allie Nash Young Organs (Fig. 242) Walter Holtkamp, senior member of the company that built and installed the new organs, said in 1959 that the large organ was one of only two so far designed with part of the pipe assembly cantilevered over the choir loft. This gives a difference in sonority. Visually it creates a striking sculptural form, enhanced by the color and texture of the pipes, which are made of copper, zinc, spotted metal, and wood. The main organ has 3 manuals, 38 stops, and 2,379 pipes; the small organ in the Meditation Chapel has 2 manuals, 12 stops, and 355 pipes.

THE CARILLON (Figs. 243, 244) The great Bourdon E-flat bell of the carillon bears the Hollins seal, the dedication to Allie Nash Young, and "Glory to God in the highest, and on earth peace, good will towards men." The legend on the A bell: "Des montagnes de Savoie à la vallée de Virginie, je chante là," proclaims the carillon's origin, for the bells were cast by Les Fils de G. Paccard of Annecy-le-Vieux. Other bells are adorned with inscriptions from the medieval Latin hymn, *Veni Creator Spiritus,* and from Isaiah, Shakespeare, Tennyson, Schiller, St. Francis of Assisi, and Ralph Hodgson, and many are further enriched with angels or elegant border designs. The B bell bears a couplet written by Arthur Talmadge:

> As Hollins ever truth doth seek
> So I, well-cast, true tones do speak

and the C-sharp bell a couplet by Jane Winston Carpenter, '59:

> Ring, bells! and summon those who seek to share
> Their search for truth, to silence and to prayer.

The forty-seven-bell carillon, unusually large for so small a tower, was designed and installed by Arthur Bigelow, who rates it as one of his finest.

168

RIDING RINGS (Figs. 245, 246) The outdoor riding ring was now finally settled in a pasture under Tinker Mountain at the northern edge of the campus. In addition to this course, an indoor ring with tack room and a barn with stalls for twenty-eight horses were ready for former Hungarian countess Judith Gyurky and her pupils in the fall of 1956. The aluminum, steel, and glass structure costing $50,000 was dubbed the hippodrome.

246. The indoor ring and stables

247. Programmed learning laboratory

PROGRAMMED LEARNING (Figs. 247, 248) Hollins staff members were in the vanguard of the movement toward programmed learning that sprang up in the late 1950s, following the lead of Dr. B. F. Skinner, who came from Harvard to speak at a Hollins seminar on automated teaching in 1960. In that year professors Allen Calvin and Maurice W. Sullivan assumed direction of a Hollins center for programmed material in mathematics and languages, under a contract with Encyclopedia Britannica Films (E.B.F.). Supplementing this was a grant of $68,000 received in 1959 from the Carnegie Corporation for a three-year testing of machines for foreign language instruction.

In 1961 the E.B.F. proposal that a large research center be created at Hollins aroused considerable dissension and controversy on the campus, for the compatibility of the aims of a liberal arts program with what many faculty feared might be an overwhelming commercial venture was questioned. The board of trustees finally turned down the proposal, and E.B.F. moved on to Palo Alto.

Remaining at Hollins was the modest cinderblock Hill Building, which E.B.F. had erected behind the old parsonage and which was to be used for foreign language offices and equipment. The Carnegie research program continued under the direction of Professor Fernand Marty, who developed a highly effective, nationally recognized programmed teaching method for foreign languages.

248. Hill Building, the Parsonage, and the Cocke Cemetery

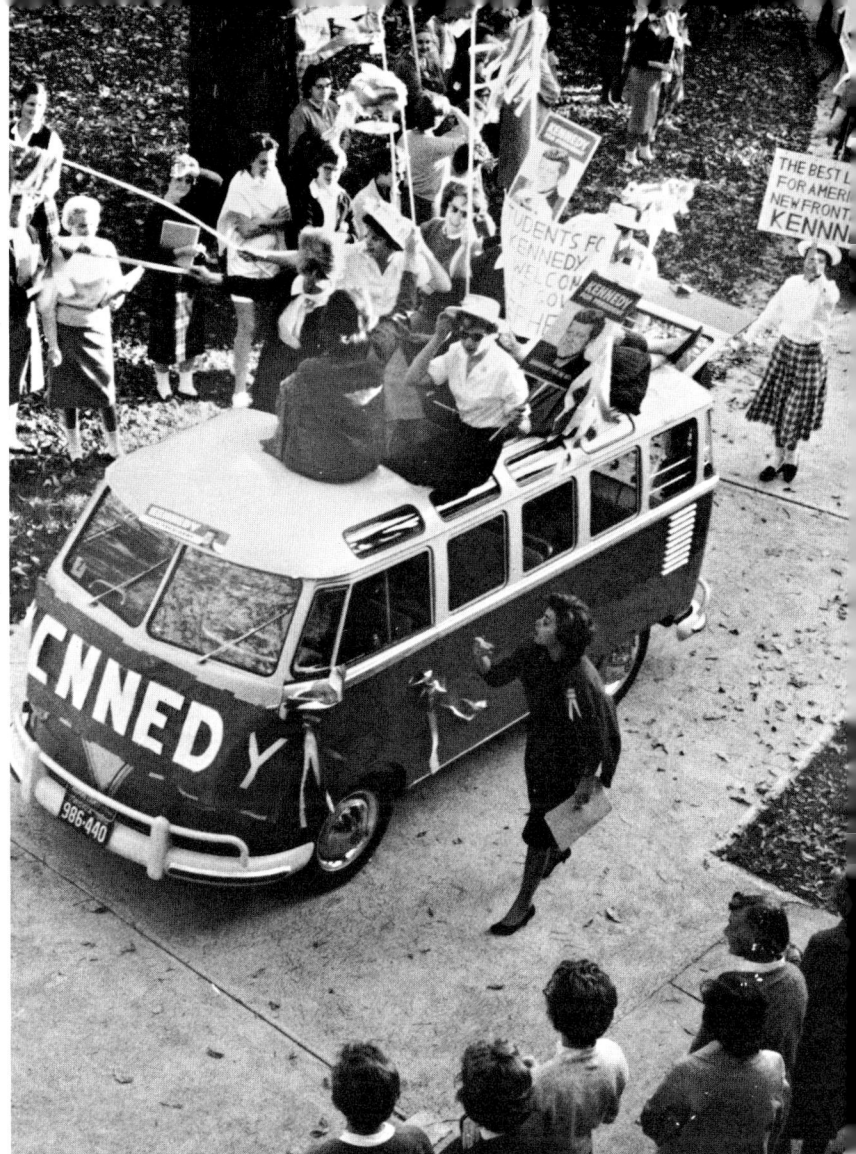

249. Kennedy-Nixon political rally, 1960

250. Christian Council holds Easter egg hunt, 1960

STUDENT ORGANIZATIONS (Figs. 249, 250) Most of the organizations that existed in 1950 continued through the decade, but there were a few changes. The honorary Writers' Club was replaced in 1954 by Grapheon, which was originally organized in 1952 to improve the campus newspaper. In 1955 students voted to disband the YWCA, which since 1888 had been autonomous, and to create a Hollins Christian Council, with chairmen elected by the entire student body. The International Relations Club sponsored the successful mock election of 1956, in which year clubs for Young Democrats and Young Republicans were first chartered at Hollins. I.R.C. disbanded in 1958, but in its place rose the Forum for those "whose interests lie in national, international, and political affairs." Again a mock election was held in 1960, with Kennedy girls and Lieutenant Governor Stephens joining in a "grand old-fashioned outdoor rally."

251. Arthur Tuden and Babatunde A. Williams

FOUNDER'S DAY (Figs. 251, 252) Freya, suggesting an all-campus academic Founder's Day, sponsored in 1952 "The Liberal Arts Curriculum at Hollins," with Dean Raushenbush of Sarah Lawrence as speaker. In succeeding years Divisions planned similar programs.

In 1954 and 1958 there were Contemporary Arts Festivals. The first included lectures by Elizabeth Bowen and Philip R. Adams, an exhibit of paintings by Charles Smith, and Hollins's first dance-drama, Olga Gratch's *Daughters of Jorio,* choreographed by Dean Goodsell. The second brought the Claremont String Quartet and the Litz-Harrison Dance Group, with composer Herbert Elwell as keynote speaker.

In 1955 the social scientists chose "Freedom around the World" as a theme, inviting President Gideonse of Brooklyn College, Frank P. Graham as U.N. representative from India and Pakistan, Erico Verissimo of Brazil, F. O. Onipede of Nigeria, and Shoa Chuan Leng of China. In 1961 a program on "Emergent Africa" included talks by L. Gray Cowan of Columbia, economist William A. Hance, anthropologist Arthur Tuden, and Nigerian political scientist Babatunde A. Williams.

In 1956 the humanities division planned its program around the dedication of the Fishburn Library. And in 1957 for "The Role of the Sciences in Promoting Peace and World-Wide Cooperation," there came Maurice Shapiro, cosmic ray specialist, Walter Whitman, secretary-general of the 1955 Geneva Conference on Peaceful Uses of Atomic Energy, and a panel of other scientists who discussed the coming International Geophysical Year.

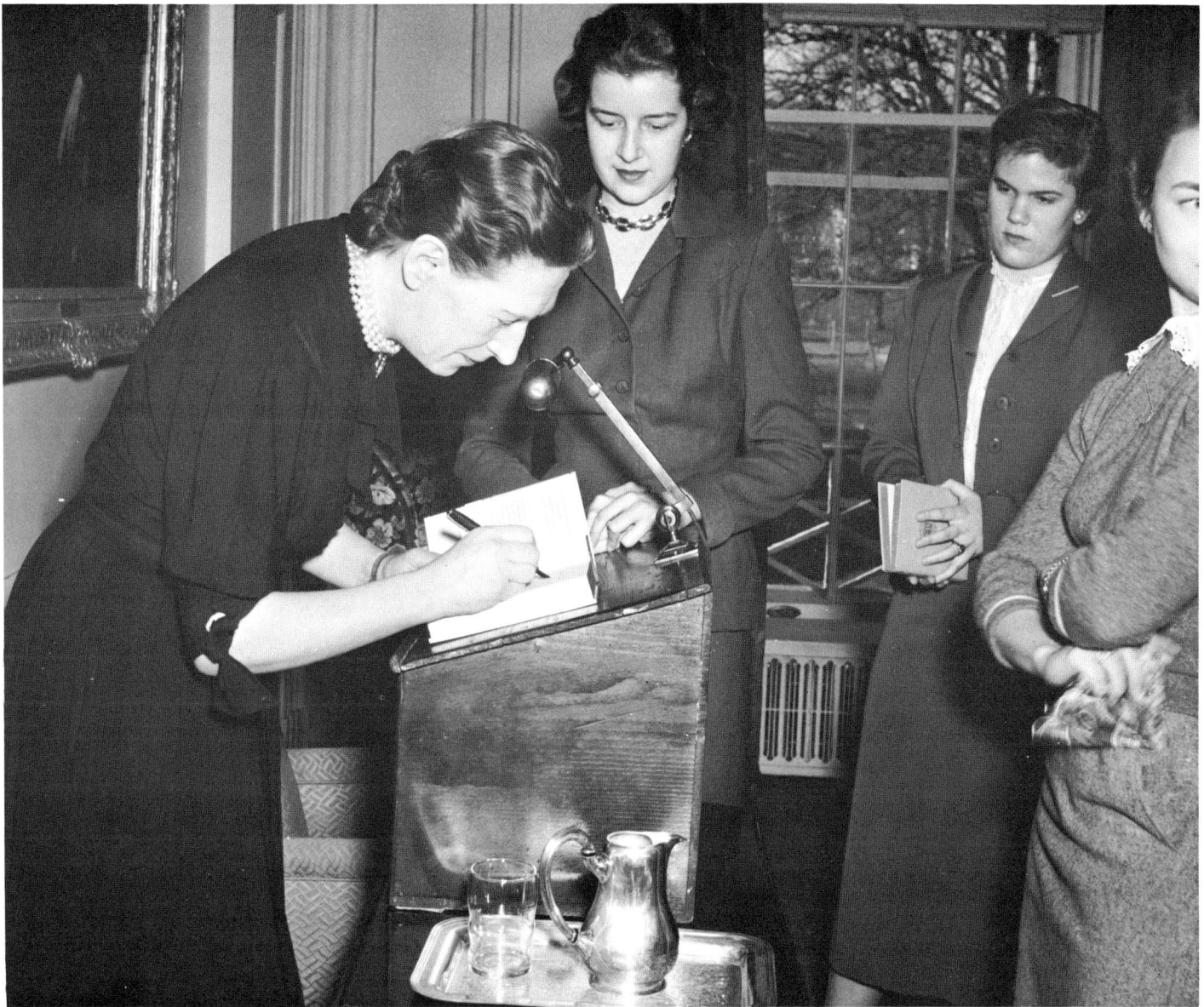

252. Elizabeth Bowen

TRADITIONS (Figs. 253–256) Undoubtedly most popular of the traditions that persisted through the decade was Tinker Day, to which seniors lately added a novel note by driving their festooned cars around the quadrangle and up the back road to the summit. May Day events were now supervised by faculty committees rather than by Freya, and added were a riding show and an informal cotillion. Christmas celebrations continued, with gifts sent far and wide: in 1960, for instance, to the World University, World Wildlife Federation, MEDICO, and the East Harlem Protestant Parish Church. Cotillion, for a while dormant, revived in 1955 to sponsor the first of annual gala dance weekends in November. There was now no place on campus large enough to hold the expanded student body; so dances accompanied by name bands and rationed liquor were held in Roanoke hotels. In sports, riding, swimming, and dance were favored, and after 1957 Odd-Even hockey and Red-Blue basketball games disappeared from the list of traditions in the student handbooks.

253. Tinker Day, 1950

254. May Day, 1953

255. Cotillion, 1956

256. Class Night, 1957

HAMBONES (Fig. 257) Enlivening the campus scene during the Everett era and for some years after were the performances of a group known as the Hollins Hambones. The *Columns* in April 1960 heralded an approaching concert thus: "The 'fabulous and frantic four' men of jazz—Willie 'Wildcat' James, Tommy 'Howlin' Hanna, Louis 'Loose' Rubin, and 'Roarin' Ralph Steinhardt—have the equivocal distinction of being the one and only band that Hollins College has ever fostered. . . . Dean 'Jazzy John' Wheeler will be master of ceremonies. Guest stars will include 'Jumpin John' Aldridge on the drums and 'Wild Bill' Carter on the trumpet."

258.   Parents' Day, 1971

PARENTS' DAY (Fig. 258) The first Parents' Day was held on April 23, 1955, with 91 guests attending a round of classes, social events, and talks by President Everett and others to enlighten parents on curricular and financial matters. By 1958 Hollins was host to over 230 visitors, and the day, expanded to a weekend, became a college tradition.

259. Commencement, 1959

COMMENCEMENT (Fig. 259) The first outdoor commencement, held on June 2, 1957, for ninety-one graduates, set the pattern for all succeeding ones. The low bank in front of East Building served as stage, and graduates and faculty processed from West. Gone were the ice-cream and lemonade stands of earlier festivities, but graduates and guests enjoyed sumptuous al fresco lunches on back campus in the interval between baccalaureate and commencement.

Class Night continued as before, but the daisy chain vanished in 1960 because of the dearth of daisies in nearby fields. Seniors in 1970 ran in with gay balloons.

VIII. Evolution in the 1960s

Presidency of John A. Logan, Jr., 1961–

D R. JOHN A. LOGAN, JR., visiting Hollins as president-elect in April 1961, remarked to reporters that "whatever we do is going to be evolutionary, not revolutionary." Succeeding events were to bear him out, and he was to guide the college through a decade of fairly rapid evolution. The role of Hollins as microcosm of the greater world is probably clearer for this decade than for any earlier period, because the college, like the nation, experienced the obsolescence of many long-accepted academic practices and social mores. In 1967 President Logan explained to alumnae, "We live in a time of greatly accelerated change." Certainly if any year in the history of Hollins were chosen as a turning point, it could well be this 125th anniversary year, for Hollins was markedly changed from 1967 on. Nevertheless, the process was one of evolution, because the seemingly drastic change to new ideas and customs was occasioned by forces and movements that often had a long history.

When John A. Logan, Jr., a native of Chicago, took office on July 1, 1961, he was well prepared for an administrative career and already established as an authority on American diplomatic history. He had completed his freshman year at Yale when he enlisted in the army in 1942, to serve at home and abroad and to advance from private to captain. In 1946 he returned to Yale, completing a B.A. degree with highest honors and continuing to an M.A. in 1951 and a Ph.D. in 1954. When selected in December 1960, as Hollins's new president, Dr. Logan was an assistant professor of history at his alma mater, and the Yale University Press was about to publish his book, *The No-Transfer Principle: a Fundamental American Security Policy.*

Experienced members of the board of trustees at the beginning of President Logan's tenure included several who were to remain at least until 1967. These were Chairman C. Francis Cocke, Vice-Chairman Alfred D. Barksdale, Mrs. Alfred I. duPont, Mrs. Barton W. Morris, Mrs. George Scott Shackelford, Jr., J. Harvie Wilkinson, Cyrus R. Osborn, Frank W. Rogers, Lewis F. Powell, Stuart T. Saunders, and English Showalter. Willard N. James remained as

secretary-treasurer to the board. Retired by 1966 were Dr. Francis P. Gaines, Mrs. Charles R. Younts, and Miss Susanna Turner. New members elected between 1962 and 1967 were John W. Hancock, Jr., of Roanoke, A. Paul Funkhouser of Philadelphia, John M. Young of New York City, Mrs. Mary Moody Northen of Galveston, Edwin W. Benjamin of New Orleans, and alumnae representatives Mrs. Osbourne O. Ashworth of Richmond, Mrs. James F. Hoge of New York City, and Mrs. Hunter B. Andrews of Hampton, Virginia.

Key members of the administration and heads of academic divisions were also to remain stable for several years. These included Vice-President Willard N. James, deans Mary Phlegar Smith and John P. Wheeler, and professors George Gordh, Kathleen Jackson, Paul Patterson, and Kermit Hunter. In January 1965 Margery Somers Foster came to succeed Dean Smith, who had stayed on for an interim semester after her retirement in 1964. Other officers who remained were Ann Splitstone, director of admission; Margaret L. Eldridge, registrar; and Carolyn Moseley, associate dean.

In 1966, after five years of the new administration, there remained also some twenty-two of the thirty-two tenured faculty members who had welcomed President Logan. Fourteen of the original thirty-four nontenured members were still at Hollins; most of these had been promoted. There were now eighty faculty members in all, plus two visiting professors.

Of faculty newly appointed between 1961 and 1966, those from Division I who were still at Hollins in 1971 included Laura Ann Laidlaw and Bettie L. Forte in classical languages, Theresia Reimers in German, William Ritter in Spanish, Jacques Bossière in French, Lawrence Becker and Allie Frazier in philosophy and religion, and Julia Randall Sawyer, Richard Dillard, and Frank O'Brien in English. Remaining in Division II were Bernard Jump and Mary D. Houska in economics, Henry Nash and Sharon Boen Webster in politics, and James Crooks in history; in Division III, Alice Bull in biology, Ronald Webster in psychology, and

David Weinman in statistics; in Division IV, David Holmes in music, and Thomas Atkins and James Ayres in drama; and in physical education, Lanetta Ware.

During this period William J. Carter was named business manager and William W. Traylor superintendent of buildings and grounds. Virginia L. Carter returned to direct the office of information and publications, and William R. Emerson came to assume the new post of assistant to the president, and Adele C. Giles to serve as the president's secretary. Mrs. Susie L. Wray became coordinator of special events, and Mrs. Frances C. Gates was active in the student activities office and eventually became its director. Staff members at Hollins throughout the decade included Jack B. Woodson, steward and then supervisor of food services; Howard M. Sexton, chef; Blanche M. Buterbaugh, manager of the secretarial services office; and Eleanor D. Mann and Ellen S. Pillow, successive managers of the Hollins Book Shop.

There was little change in the academic structure of Hollins through these first five years. The catalogues carried the earlier statement of college aims, and the requirements for the B.A. and for major studies remained generally the same. A new undergraduate research program in sciences was begun in 1961, and a German major was added in 1962. In 1963 American area studies were reinstated, the separate disciplines of philosophy and religion again merged to form one department, and students were given the option of enrolling in a United Nations Semester sponsored by Drew University.

Social changes were also few in number in these early years. Honor court concerned itself now only with cases involving lying, cheating, and stealing; a judicial court took care of other infractions of rules. Students were finally permitted to smoke in their rooms but were expected to obey new rules restricting sunbathing locations. Sunday chapel service was no longer required from 1962 on, but students had to be present at Wednesday night services and at convocations.

During this apparent lull, however, a great deal of planning was in progress. President Logan and the board of trustees had agreed that, for most efficient operation of the college, enrollment should be expanded to about one thousand students. Future needs had to be analyzed, plans drawn, and costs estimated. In 1962 the firm of Taylor, Lieberfeld, and Heldman, Inc., educational consultants, made a study of the space needed by every college department, and the resulting Lieberfeld Report served as basis for the first plans for college expansion. By May 1963 the New Haven firm of Douglas Orr, deCossy, Winder, and Associates had completed a topographical survey of the campus, and six months later the same firm had a master plan ready for formal presentation. This plan was created under the direct supervision of Douglas Orr, former president of the American Institute of Architects, member of the National Fine Arts Commission, and consulting architect for Princeton, Yale, and Bryn Mawr. As President Logan's father-in-law, Orr took an intimate interest in Hollins.

Three new major buildings were envisioned: a dormitory, a science building, and a college center. Projected also were new wings for the Fishburn Library and the Little Theatre, renovation of Pleasants Building and the power house, and a new president's home. Since the cost of the three immediately necessary major buildings was calculated to be close to $8 million, another survey was made to judge Hollins's fund-raising potential. The report from this having proved optimistic, a major capital fund campaign was launched by the board of trustees in 1964. Board members Cyrus R. Osborn and Mrs. George Scott Shackelford agreed to serve as cochairmen for this first drive, which had as its goal the raising of $10 million. And there was great excitement when construction of the new dormitory was begun in 1965, with the fortunate aid of a loan from the College Facilities Division of the Housing and Home Finance Agency.

Meanwhile there was no academic lull, for an institutional self-study made in 1962–63 for the Southern Association of Colleges and Secondary Schools involved the energies of administration, faculty, and students and provided the base upon which to build a new academic program. Active work on the New Curriculum began in 1964 under the enthusiastic chairmanship of Professor Janet MacDonald and the eager sponsorship of the new dean, Dr. Margery Foster. Questionnaires, committees, subcommittees, reports, debates, concessions seemed to increase geometrically over a two-year period, until many members of the Hollins community felt that nothing in the past had ever been so thoroughly dissected. Constantly on agenda were discussions of requirements, teaching methods, calendars for the year and for the week, improvement of the freshman year and of the senior year, and a multitude of other topics. As debates led to resolutions, Hollins was embarking on its 125th anniversary year.

The year was celebrated in stages, from Founder's Day of 1967 to Founder's Day of 1968. The decision to commemorate the close of a century and a quarter of women's education by presenting newly coined medals to outstanding women met with approval; so there were festive days not only on February 21 but during graduation weekend in 1967, when more alumnae could share in the celebrating.

There were other causes for celebration. One was that Hollins was one of twenty-five women's colleges given $10,000 grants by Time, Inc., "for academic excellence and leadership," and in recognition of Hollins alumnae working for Time publications. Another was publicized by the Hollins brochure, *125th Anniversary Goals.* Within a decade the average faculty salary had increased by 77 percent and full professors had enjoyed an 87 percent increase (from an average of $8,007 to one of $14,995). The optimum enrollment predicted for 1961 had already been reached—the 1967–68 session opened with a total of 1,004 undergraduate and graduate students. Enrollments within classes were nicely balanced, with 262 freshmen, 277 sophomores, 242 juniors, and 204 seniors. By the fall of 1967 the new dormitory, Tinker House, was a year old, and the new science building, to be named Dana, was almost completely ready for classes. New also that September were curriculum, class schedule, academic calendar. A new student government constitution had been effective since January. Those few faculty members who had been away from cam-

pus on sabbatical leaves felt that they were returning to a different college, even though they had seen the early stages of this evolution, partly because there were so many new faces to be seen at the opening faculty meeting.

There was also a new format for the Hollins College catalogue, in which a revised statement of the college's aims appeared during the anniversary year. It read as follows:

The founder of Hollins College, Charles Lewis Cocke, dedicated it to "the cultivation of sound learning, virtuous feelings, and independent thought." These high objectives, together with a conviction that they are best achieved through a study of the liberal arts and sciences, are as descriptive of the aims of a Hollins education today as they were over a century and a quarter ago. Curriculum and social regulations evolve in response to new ideas and changing times, but fundamental purposes endure.

Hollins College is a community of scholars engaged in evaluating, communicating, preserving, and enlarging mankind's store of knowledge. To this end, the college endeavors to create an environment which generates a love of learning, habits of critical thought and accurate expression and, ultimately, the strength of character and spiritual values needed for a productive life in modern society.

Succeeding catalogues carried also the central statement of the new curriculum:

We believe that a college is the institution uniquely qualified to offer the rigorous study of subject matter which makes possible a mastery of the process of learning, that learning improves as the individual becomes more deeply involved in her own education, and that, in view of the growth of knowledge, the needs of the individual student can best be met by flexibility and a minimum of requirements.

Briefly stated, the requirements for the B.A. degree under this new scheme sounded very much like the old ones. Each student was required to take a colloquium; a course in humanities and another in related fields; two courses in the social sciences; two in the fine arts; and two in laboratory science, mathematics, or statistics. She still had to show proficiency in a foreign language and satisfy requirements in physical education.

The former policy of requiring the same core of general education for all students, however, was now modified to allow each one to plan a program tailored to her particular abilities and interests. There was a much wider range of choice among courses, with the possibility of exemption from some and of admission with advanced standing to others. There were multiple alternatives among the colloquia—discussion courses—in which freshmen were enrolled. Students normally took four courses each semester, rather than five, in order to do more intensive study. Seniors were expected to concentrate on independent work, either in research projects or within small seminar groups. To the traditional major programs were added options for extra-departmental majors, such as the Russian studies and the English-French literature major offered in 1967. In 1970 there appeared also a college major, which focused upon a period, an idea, or an issue. Such flexibility was encouraged with the hope, as Dean Foster expressed it, "that the opportunity for independence will encourage in each student the habit of finding and evaluating material for herself."

Each Hollins girl was strongly encouraged to do so during the new short term that was inserted in the middle of the academic year. Fall and spring semesters were reduced to twelve weeks from the former fifteen, and mid-year examinations were given before Christmas vacation. The whole of January, then, might be devoted to intensive pursuit of one project, either at Hollins or afield. Short-term courses were offered on campus, but increasingly students chose to go elsewhere, and also to combine learning with vocational experience. The viability and the popularity of the "mini-mester" have proved Hollins's discernment in pioneering in this program.

By 1971 minor changes had been made in the now four-year-old curriculum, and more options were available. To the earlier off-campus programs were added one at the University of East Anglia in Norwich, England, and another at Trinity College in Dublin, Ireland. An Eight College Consortium allowed Hollins girls to attend classes for a semester or a year at Davidson, Hampden-Sydney, Randolph-Macon, Sweet Briar, Mary Baldwin, and Randolph-Macon Woman's colleges, or at Washington and Lee University. (The majority of Hollins girls taking such leaves chose to try coeducation.) Hollins students could also now plan their own examination schedules under a system inaugurated and administered by their colleagues, and they could enroll in a certain number of courses under a pass-fail option, eschewing the traditional letter grades. No-cut days before and after vacations were by now abolished.

Greater freedom, however, often brought greater endeavor. Graduates had been winning Woodrow Wilson and other fellowships in increasing numbers, and many seniors were anticipating graduate study. Departmental honors, first offered under the new curriculum and first awarded to sixteen graduates in 1968, became increasingly desirable. And, obviously, students who merited academic freedom and responsibility and who were expected to exercise self-discipline and judgment and to develop analytical and critical attitudes were going to bring other changes to Hollins community life.

The sense of community that had always characterized Hollins remained strong through the 1960s. It was often manifested, however, in a manner so different from that of previous decades that it was not always recognized or commended. All-campus convocations were now rare. Their occurrence seemed to imply momentous rather than routine occasions, and they did occur in times of great urgency, as during the nationwide turmoil aroused by the tragic killing of students at Kent State University in May 1970. Questions such as What should the community do? or How should the community act? were answered in large measure by the students, who felt that their stake in their education was larger than the share of faculty and administration. President Logan commented in the *Bulletin* of March 1966 on these "activists of the 1960's" who were "brighter than any previous generation, idealistic, relatively unkempt and nonconformist, eager that not only they but their colleagues be engaged in the great issues of the times." College generations of these years were basically sober and idealistic, but they were shocked by incredible assassinations, beset by problems of poverty and racism, by ecological threats, by undeclared war in Vietnam and unwanted intervention in Cambodia. And they were impatient, wanting to discard the slow working of social and political change, seeking their ideal goals by immediate action. Needing to retain their individuality, insisting on the independence of their life-styles, they still wanted group action, and it was difficult for many of them to understand that the college, as an entity, had to guarantee democratic freedoms and could not foster political action.

The last general Student Government Association meeting was held in December 1966. Already the Little Theatre was too small to hold the 926 undergraduates enrolled for the session, and from now on senators were to represent varied groups of constituents. A new S.G.A. constitution, made effective in January 1967 and revised in May 1970, confirmed a new honor and community trust system. An honor court continued to deal with violations involving lying, cheating, and stealing, while a dormitory life committee handled infractions of other rules. There were, in fact, few regulations listed in the *Hollins Index,* which in 1971 superseded the former *Handbooks.* Pets other than goldfish or turtles were prohibited; sunbathing on roofs and balconies and smoking in assembly rooms or corridors were forbidden; parietal hours were limited. The statement that "students may not keep firearms on campus" recalled the 1840s. But contemporary concerns were mirrored by the Virginia state laws quoted in the final pages of the *Index,* which governed illegal use of drugs and alcoholic beverages, abortion, speeding, and hitchhiking.

The Student Government Association retained a complex organization, and by 1971 it was administering a large budget. Major allocations of the total of $47,037 included $13,200 for the *Spinster,* $9,500 for *Hollins Columns,* and $3,790 for a foreign student scholarship. The association was not shirking responsibility, and the declining number of

social regulations was not to be viewed in a negative light. The accent throughout the Honor and Community Trust System was a positive one. In essence, it called for consideration of the reputation of the college, respect for the life of the community, and concern for the privacy of the individual.

It also opened the way toward another ideal: the concept of community government. Students had long hoped to share in the formulating of college policy, to act with faculty and administration on committees, to have voting privileges. They had been evaluating their courses and their teachers by informal and formal questionnaires for some years before their publication of the first *Hollins Course Critique* in 1971. Since 1969 student representatives had come to departmental and divisional meetings, and students who wished to attend faculty meetings were welcomed to the extent of the available seats in Bradley or Babcock auditoriums. Finally, after two years of discussion, faculty and students voted affirmatively for community government, and their vote was ratified by the board of trustees in February 1972, becoming effective on the following May 1. Provisions of community government included the establishment of a common college legislature, composed of all teaching faculty and others with equivalent status, two alumnae members chosen by the alumnae association, and enough students to comprise 25 percent of the total membership. The conferring of Hollins degrees and the advising of the president on specific matters of appointment and tenure were to remain under sole faculty control, and there were to be no student members on the faculty's committee on conference with the trustees. All other standing committees, however, were to reflect a communal sharing, with student or faculty groups retaining the privilege of meeting separately on occasion.

One reason these changes progressed as smoothly as they did may be that the faculty group itself had changed considerably in these later years of the decade. Of the eighty-five full-time faculty members at Hollins in September 1971, only twenty-three had been at Hollins since 1961. The forty-six teachers appointed after 1966 had, in effect, come in with the new curriculum. Appointed to upper faculty rank between 1966 and 1971 were professors William Jay Smith and George P. Garrett in English, and associate professors Nathan J. Kranowski in French and Charles Morlang, Jr., in biology. Dr. J. C. Zillhardt came as college physician, and Richard E. Kirkwood as librarian. In 1971 only 70 percent of the faculty held the Ph.D. degree, in contrast to the 80 percent of 1966, but this was in part due to the fact that all of the thirty-five assistant professors and the eleven instructors had come to Hollins since 1966, and many were in the process of completing their doctorates. There was an equivalent turnover in the position of associate dean for student life, with three incumbents up to 1970, when the post was assumed by alumna Baylies Hearon Willey, '57. A new role, that of associate dean for student academic affairs, was taken by David W. Holmes, and Helen S. Goodsell took charge of the growing office of director of student aid and vocational guidance. In 1967 John P. Wheeler succeeded Margery S. Foster as dean of the college.

Constituency of the board of trustees changed also, because half of its members joined the board after the 125th anniversary year. In 1968 both C. Francis Cocke and Judge Barksdale resigned their offices, and Cyrus R. Osborn was elected chairman and English Showalter vice-chairman. After Osborn's sudden death during the year, Showalter became chairman, aided by vice-chairmen John W. Hancock, Jr. (1969–70) and Robert B. Claytor (from 1970 on). New members included Mrs. F. Otto Haas of Ambler, Pennsylvania, Frank Batten of Norfolk, Dr. Harold B. Whiteman, Jr., and Mrs. James F. Hoge of New York City, Mrs. Leslie Cheek, Jr., of Richmond, Mrs. Gardner W. Bond, Jr., of Bedford, Virginia, and from Roanoke, Benjamin F. Parrott, Robert B. Claytor, George B. Cartledge, Sr., and Frank W. Rogers, Jr. Alumnae representatives on the board included Mrs. Sion A. Boney of Greensboro, North Carolina, Mrs. Robert N. Fishburn of Roanoke, and Mrs. Lee M. Kenna of Charleston, West Virginia.

Many problems confronted President Logan and his board of trustees, and they became increasingly grave during the late 1960s. Practically all could have been surmounted were sufficient sums forthcoming. (One wryly recalls Charles Lewis Cocke's comparison of Hollins's funds with those of Vassar in the 1860s when contrasting Hollins's endowment in the 1960s with those of comparable colleges, regretting this form of continuity.) Hollins's endowment remained woefully small, being in 1971 even slightly under the $7 million value of five years earlier. Meanwhile costs were skyrocketing. The total operational budget of $1,714,441 for 1960–61 was tripled in the $5,290,000 budget for 1971–72. Tuition, room, and board charges rose during the same period from $2,300 to $3,750, and it was not possible to meet the urgent requests for scholarships. Even though financial aid to students doubled between 1967 and 1971, with scholarships, work-pay, and loans rising to a total of $587,625 and 28 percent of the incoming freshmen receiving aid, more was needed. Large federal grants were dwindling, and corporations and private donors were suffering from the national economic uncertainties. At Hollins, admission applications were decreasing in number and attrition rates were rising. All private colleges, and many public ones, were also suffering financial stress, but Hollins's problems were no less acute even if shared.

The original dream of a ten-year expansion program had faded years before 1971, for costs had accelerated beyond all expectation. The goal of the capital funds campaign was revised upward, reaching by 1971 $18 million. Chairmanship of the campaign passed in 1968 to Stuart T. Saunders, aided by A. Paul Funkhouser and Mrs. Charles P. Orr. Active resumption of the campaign, however, awaited a hoped-for brightening of the nation's economic condition.

Happily, half of the originally projected dormitory existed in Tinker House, and Dana Science Building had been completed. Carvin's Creek had been moved, the power plant had been renovated, and there were new roads and new tennis courts. Pleasants Hall, now housing offices and classrooms for social sciences, classical languages, and several other disciplines, was refurbished and colorful, as were the

Little Theatre and the president's office in the Cocke Memorial Building. Acquisition of a recently built apartment complex and two other properties across the highway provided for lodging an overflow of students and faculty. To the retirement benefits and the major medical and group life insurance made available to faculty through the Teachers Insurance and Annuity Association were added in the 1960s the TIAA total disability benefits and options for accidental dismemberment and group automobile insurance plans. Employees were fully covered by social security and participated in Blue Cross–Blue Shield benefits through a group plan. Appreciated also by many faculty families was the faculty children's tuition plan established in 1962.

Projected as the next major building on campus was the college center. A link with the older Hollins was made with the decision to dedicate this structure to the late William Lewis Moody, Jr., and his wife, Libbie Rice Shearn Moody. William Moody, at the age of nine, was sent to stay with the Pleasants family and to attend classes at Hollins Institute from 1874 to 1877, because his father had roomed with "Uncle Billy" Pleasants at the University of Virginia. Later, having graduated from V.M.I., the young Moody embarked on a business career, becoming an eminent Texas financier and philanthropist. His daughter, Mrs. Mary Moody Northen of Galveston, civic leader and educational benefactor, joined the Hollins board of trustees in 1965 and later generously pledged $800,000 toward the cost of the student center. The Moody Center is to include dining rooms, lounges, bookshop, and other facilities. Already named are the faculty dining room honoring Mary Stuart Cocke Goodwin, '06, the alumnae lounge honoring Mary Rowland Perkinson, '28, a museum endowed by a generous gift from Billie Camp Younts, '16, and a recreation room in memory of Joan Banta, '69. A faculty lounge and an art gallery are to be named respectively for the late professors F. Lamar Janney and John R. Ballator. Grants toward the Moody Center include one of $30,000 from the Lilly Endowment, Inc., of Indianapolis, another of $100,000 from the Haas Commu-

nity Fund established by Dr. and Mrs. F. Otto Haas of Philadelphia, and a third of $250,000 from the Charles A. Dana Foundation.

There were, however, many frustrating delays in the execution of the college's plans for expansion. By the end of 1971 plans of the Moody Center were being revised to lower the cost of its construction. Fishburn Library, with some 25,000 volumes added since 1967, no longer had adequate space for books or for their readers, and the planned extension was delayed, as was the planned wing for the Little Theatre. Equally distressing was the delay in the erection of a new president's home, for which present and former members of the board of trustees had donated money late in 1968. These projects awaited the second phase of the capital funds campaign. A future third phase would, hopefully, greatly strengthen Hollins's permanent endowment.

On the positive side, there was encouraging productivity from Hollins's community of scholars. Funds for Hollins's research and travel committee remained stable at $10,000 annually. But there were welcomed extras. The psychology department still received the largest subsidies, and its professors, all engaged in basic research, garnered over a million dollars in federal funds in the decade between 1959 and 1969. A National Science Foundation grant for a College Science Improvement Program, familiarly known as COSIP, offered $143,600 to be used over a three-year period by sociologists, economists, and political scientists as well as by members of the mathematics and science departments. In 1968 a grant of $50,000 from the Ford Foundation, to be matched by Hollins and to be administered over a four-year period, aided teachers in humanities, fine arts, and history, and in March 1971 Hollins received a $200,-000 grant from the Andrew W. Mellon Foundation to be used for faculty development, primarily in the area of the humanities. These large grants were accompanied by numerous smaller ones, all of which were highly appreciated by faculty members.

The total creative activity of Hollins's full-time teaching

faculty during this decade of President Logan's administration would be remarkable even for a larger college. In one aspect alone—publication—there was impressive productivity. Articles appearing in scholarly journals and essays and poems in collections are too numerous to list, but published books indicate the wide range of types and subjects covered by Hollins authors.

Texts include Fernand Marty's *Active French Foundation Course,* his *Linguistics Applied to the Beginning French Course,* and his *Teaching French;* Lowell Wine's *Statistics for Scientists and Engineers;* Paul Woods's *Workbook to Accompany Psychology;* Allie Frazier's *Issues in Religion;* Barbara Hargrove's *Reformation of the Holy: a Sociology of Religion;* and F. Joseph McGuigan's *Experimental Psychology,* his *Biological Basis of Behavior,* and his *Thinking: Studies of Covert Language Processes.* Anthologies edited by Hollins faculty members include John A. Allen's *Hero's Way: Contemporary Poems in the Mythic Tradition;* Frank O'Brien's collection of poetry written in Irish, *Dŭanaire Nuafhiliocht;* the Russian critical essays in *Literature and National Identity,* coedited by Jesse Zeldin; *The Idea of an American Novel* by John Moore and Louis Rubin; Donald White's *Medieval History: a Source Book;* the readings in American social and cultural history edited by Richard Dillard and Louis Rubin under the title *The Experience of America;* Allie Frazier's *Readings in Eastern Religious Thought* in three volumes, including *Hinduism, Buddhism,* and *Chinese and Japanese Religions;* and the three-volume anthology of *Russian Philosophy* coedited by Mary-Barbara Zeldin.

Among critical studies may be listed John Moore's analysis of Yeats's plays in his *Masks of Love and Death;* Jacques Bossière's publication of Charles Du Bos's *Du Spirituel dans l'Ordre Litteraire;* Jesse Zeldin's edition of Nikolai Gogol's *Selected Passages from Correspondence with Friends;* Mary-Barbara Zeldin's edition of Peter Yakovlevich Chaadayev's *Philosophical Letters and Apology of a Madman;* Frank O'Brien's prize-winning study of literature in Irish, *Filíocht*

Ghaeilge Na Linne Seo; Louis Rubin's *The Faraway Country: Writers of the Modern South, The Teller and the Tale,* and *The Curious Death of the Novel;* and Thomas Hanna's *The Lyrical Existentialists, The Bergsonian Heritage,* and *The Thought and Art of Albert Camus.*

Cultural and intellectual histories include Robert Ramsey's *Carolina Cradle,* on early settlers of the North Carolina frontier; Frances Niederer's architectural and social history of *The Town of Fincastle, Virginia;* George Gordh's *Christian Faith and Its Cultural Expression,* which took the duPont Chapel as one of its major examples; Herta Freitag's *The Number Story,* written with her husband at the request of the National Council of Teachers of Mathematics; James B. Crooks's study of urban progressivism in Baltimore, entitled *Politics and Progress;* and Bettie Forte's *Rome and the Romans as the Greeks Saw Them,* published under the auspices of the American Academy in Rome.

This was also a notable decade for poetry. Among books by Hollins poets were Julia Randall Sawyer's *The Puritan Carpenter* and her *Adam's Dream;* Richard Dillard's *The Day I Stopped Dreaming about Barbara Steele* and his *News of the Nile;* George Garrett's *For a Bitter Season;* John A. Allen's *The Lean Divider;* and William Jay Smith's *The Tin Can and Other Poems* and his *New and Collected Poems.* Also, Professor Smith was appointed to the prestigious post of Consultant in Poetry to the Library of Congress during this decade. *Hollins Poets,* an anthology published by the University Press of Virginia, includes poems by professors Sawyer, Smith, Dillard, and Allen, and by Jean Farley. Novels written at Hollins included not only Louis Rubin's *The Golden Weather* and George Garrett's *The Death of the Fox,* but also several by students, such as Anna Sevier's *Early Summer,* Sylvia Wilkinson's *Moss on the North Side,* and Lee Smith's *The Last Day the Dogbushes Bloomed.*

Notable among Hollins's own publications was *The Hollins Critic,* a national literary journal inaugurated in 1964 by an editorial board headed by Louis Rubin and John Moore. Essays from this appeared in 1971 in the book, *The*

Sounder Few, published by the University of Georgia Press. Notable also for their frequent winning of national awards were the various Hollins bulletins edited by Virginia L. Carter and designed by Ronald L. Seichrist.

The preceding lists of literary productions should not, however, outweigh other scholarly and creative activities. These are too numerous to mention, but some outstanding examples may be cited. There may be noted, for instance, Ronald Webster's nationally recognized program for stutterer's self-monitoring and the research in behavior being done by professors Webster, Woods, and McGuigan; in October 1971 Hollins played host to the International Conference on the Psychophysiology of Thinking. There were Henry Nash's study of nuclear weapons and international behavior, to be published under NATO auspices, and Bernard Jump's reports for the New York State Commission on the Powers of Local Government. John Diercks composed over sixty published musical compositions and won annual ASCAP awards; Oscar McCullough concertized across the United States and in Europe; Kermit Hunter created historic dramas and Thomas Atkins several plays, and in 1971 Professor Atkins began to edit a new national quarterly, *The Film Journal*. Anne Laidlaw won an award from the American Academy in Rome for her archaeological work at Cosa and Pompeii and began annual cross-country lecture tours for the American Institute of Archaeology. There were notable exhibits of paintings by John Ballator and Lewis Thompson. Ralph Steinhardt developed a constant-temperature bath apparatus and had it patented for Hollins; he traveled to Paris to lecture on his pioneer work in spectroscopic studies. Many faculty were, in fact, lecturing at meetings around the world. John Moore was invited to Beirut to speak on Kahlil Gibran; Anne McClenny gave a lecture-recital on the early American music of Alexander Reinagle to an audience in Glasgow; Dean Goodsell lectured to theater groups in Bombay, Calcutta, and Madras. Thomas Atkins represented the United States at an International Film Festival in Florence; Mary-Barbara Zeldin read a paper at the International Congress of Philosophy in Vienna; F. Joseph McGuigan in 1969 read papers both in London and in Montevideo, Uruguay. Many others were also traveling to attend meetings or to pursue research. And analytical studies, investigations, and community projects were undertaken by a great many members of the Hollins faculty.

Among community projects sponsored by the college and inaugurated during this decade, perhaps most successful was the annual series of Wednesday morning lectures for women, known as the Hollins Winter Seminars. The lectures, suggested by Mrs. Logan and supported by local alumnae, proved popular from the beginning, both with the faculty members who spoke on diverse topics and to their sizable audiences. A similar format was followed for the Alumnae College program that was revived in 1965 and held for a few days at commencement. Then there were numerous conferences and festivals, among which the most elaborate were the annual Literary Festivals and the June 1970 Creative Writing and Cinema Conference. Countless speakers and performers were invited to Hollins by various organizations, and the weekly calendars that in 1971 supplanted the former monthly ones grew longer and longer. Audiences generally became smaller, for with increasing fragmentation of interest and multiplicity of offerings there were only rare lecturers—such as Gloria Steinem—who attracted large crowds.

A new and relatively novel graduate program, supported by the Old Dominion and the Andrew W. Mellon foundations, was introduced in 1969. Summer and a few winter courses were offered toward a degree of Master of Arts in Liberal Studies, planned primarily for elementary and secondary school teachers and librarians. The first M.A.L.S. degree was conferred in May 1970. By the fall of 1971 there were eighty-nine candidates enrolled in the program.

Hollins students, like their faculty, continued to be involved in both central and centrifugal concerns. Total enrollment figures for undergraduates had risen from the 677 of 1961 to the 1,050 of 1971, and understandably the community, more heterogeneous in nature than ever before, reflected a wide variety of interests. For example, although there had been no problem about admitting black students in the mid-1960s because the Hollins charter made no restrictions as to creed, color, or nationality, problems did arise because there were so few. Late in 1971 the twenty-five on campus, forming an organization called Concerned Black Students, planned to establish an African and Black American Culture Center in Rath Haus. There were other similar autonomous groups. The provenance of undergraduates had remained fairly constant through the decade, however, and figures from 1971 may be taken as typical. Forty-one states were represented in the student body: 22 percent from Virginia, 35 percent from elsewhere in the South, 28 percent from the Northeast, 11 percent from central and western states, and 4 percent from twenty foreign countries.

In general there was less interest in purely social clubs and events, and less participation in spectator sports. As senior Mary Beth Hatten wrote for the May 1971 *Alumnae Bulletin,* however, "In the midst of change, meaningful Hollins traditions remain to give the college community a sense of its past and a common experience to enjoy together. . . . Fun has always been a part of learning, and, for those who complain that involvement minimizes fun or that ours is a solemn generation, we offer our antics in reply." Seniors in 1971 sponsored a "hop" in Botetourt Hall, reviving the past by wearing quaint costumes of the 1950s and presenting their chaperones with corsages. Earlier, in 1966, eleven recent graduates and a few other students had floated down the Mississippi from Paducah to New Orleans on a raft named the *Rosebud Hobson* after a Hollins Kentucky girl of 1906. Small singing groups—Undertones, Accidentals, and Hollypoofs—continued to flourish, and a Gothic Festival and weekly Saturday Morning Fun Club shows enlivened the fall and winter of 1971. Long dresses and old-fashioned shirtwaists were now occasionally to be seen among the patched blue jeans and jackets of unisex style, and both faculty and younger men were sporting Victorian beards and long hair. Two-wheeled vehicles were becoming popular again; in the fall of 1971 fourteen new racks had to be purchased to hold the 150-odd bicycles on campus.

As President Logan remarked in his opening speech in September 1968, "No college exists in a vacuum, or exists solely for those who inhabit its campus at a given point in time." Both continuity and change have always characterized Hollins. More changes will come; evolution will continue. As presage of hope for the future, President Logan's concluding remarks in his address to the Newcomen Club during the 125th anniversary year are appropriate. He said:

As I look towards the future of the College, like all Hollins people I take courage from her past. Throughout her 125 years, Hollins' existence has been an act of faith. There has never been a time when the college was not threatened by one kind of danger or another—by the destruction and dislocation of the Civil War which came upon it in its earliest days, by the rigors of a Reconstruction which left the South prostrate and all her institutions shaken, and by the two great wars of this century as well as the greatest depression in modern times.

Despite all these threats to her survival, here is Hollins today, one of the oldest women's colleges in the country and one of the best, I think, flourishing as she has never done before. Problems remain and we do not deny the fact that they are grave ones. But we have dealt with problems before and mastered them, and I am confident we shall master these new problems as our predecessors did the old ones. There is ample cause to believe that our society will continue to recognize and to support the special advantages of intimacy, of style, and of excellence which colleges like Hollins offer.

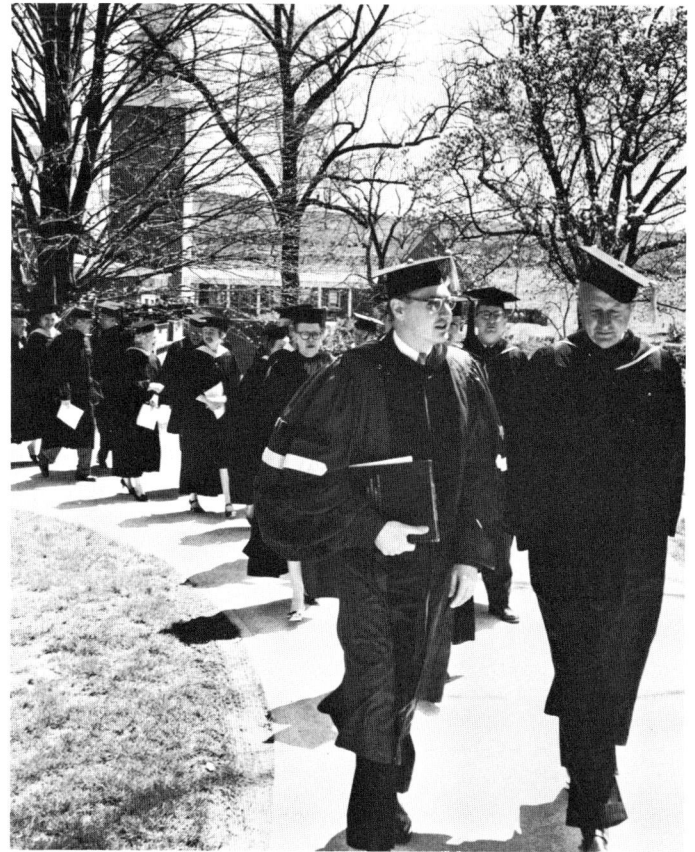

261.   Academic procession, Logan inaugural

PRESIDENT JOHN A. LOGAN, JR. (Fig. 260) President Logan, while meeting the multifaceted duties of his administrative post at Hollins, has continued working for national educational and cultural programs. Shortly before coming to Hollins, Dr. Logan taught at a Salzburg seminar in American studies. In 1962 he was called by the American Council on Education to serve on a three-man committee set up for the Department of State to encourage the international exchange of scholars. Then in 1965 he was appointed to the council's Commission on International Education, and in 1967 he went to Tunis with an inspection team to examine the cultural activities of the U.S. Embassy there.

In 1967 Dr. Logan also assumed the presidency of the Virginia Foundation of Independent Colleges and was appointed to the Physical Facilities Planning Committee of the Virginia State Council of Higher Education. In 1970 he began serving on the executive committee of the board of Independent College Funds of America, Inc., and in 1971 he was elected as the first president of the new Council of Independent Colleges in Virginia.

Intermittently President Logan has been able to indulge his interest in sports cars and jazz, playing tenor sax for the Hambones during that group's active period. Both he and his wife, Ann Orr Logan, have also maintained a tradition of gracious entertaining during their frequent travels as well as at home.

262. Eugene R. Black delivers address

INAUGURATION OF PRESIDENT LOGAN (Figs. 261, 262) Ceremonies accompanying the induction of Dr. John A. Logan, Jr., as fifth president of Hollins took place during the weekend of April 14–15, 1962. A major address was given on Saturday morning by Eugene R. Black, president of the World Bank and husband of a Hollins alumna. Then came the investiture, with C. Francis Cocke delivering the Hollins charter to the new president. Dr. Logan's speech dealt with the problems of education. "We must stress the relevance of fields of learning to one another," he said, "and particularly to the major problems and challenges of the mid-twentieth century. . . . The ultimate purpose of education is the attainment of wisdom. . . . Out of the hard intellectual effort required to master new and difficult disciplines there will remain residual habits of thought and attitudes which are the mark of an educated person—a passion for truth, for beauty, for justice and for human freedom."

A carillon recital, campus tours and exhibits, and the president's reception concluded Saturday's festivities for the numerous delegates and other guests.

The Sunday sermon, delivered by the Reverend Liston Pope, Dean of the Yale Divinity School, had as its theme "The Beginning of Knowledge." Dean Pope spoke of the immeasurable increase in knowledge, sadly accompanied by insecurity, cynicism, and skepticism, and urged a return to the belief that a college education may help to develop "positive intellectual and spiritual leadership for the world."

263. Cyrus R. Osborn

CHAIRMEN OF THE BOARD OF TRUSTEES (Figs. 263–265) Chairmanship of the board of trustees was assumed by Cyrus R. Osborn in May 1968 but all too briefly, for Osborn died in November of that year. A member of the board since 1956, he had added in 1964 the demanding role of directing the capital-funds campaign. Osborn, who maintained residences at Bloomfield Hills, Michigan, and Warm Springs, Virginia, joined the General Motors Corporation in 1917 and rose to serve as its executive vice-president and director from 1959 to 1963. In addition to his work for Hollins, Osborn served as trustee for Alma College, Michigan, and Monmouth College, Illinois.

Roanoke attorney English Showalter, elected to the Hollins board of trustees in 1956, succeeded Judge Barksdale as vice-chairman in 1968, and was elected chairman in 1969. A graduate of Lynchburg College, Showalter received his law degree from the University of Virginia. His multiple chairmanships have included those of the executive committee of the Colonial-American National Bank and of the boards of the Roanoke Valley S.P.C.A. and of two Roanoke steel companies. He has also served as director and president of the Old Dominion Fire Insurance Company of Roanoke, as president of the Roanoke Valley Community Foundation, and is a former president of the Roanoke Bar Association and the Community Fund.

Upon Showalter's retirement from the board in May 1972 Robert B. Claytor of Roanoke was elected chairman. Claytor, Phi Beta Kappa graduate of Princeton University and Harvard Law School, joined the Hollins board in 1968. Since 1951 he has been attorney for the Norfolk and Western Railway, and is now its executive vice-president. He is also a member of the boards of directors of the V.P.I. Educational Foundation, Burrell Memorial Hospital, Goodwill Industries, and the United Fund of Roanoke Valley, and serves as chancellor of the Episcopal Diocese of Southwestern Virginia.

264.   English Showalter

265.   Robert B. Claytor

DEAN MARGERY S. FOSTER (Fig. 266) Dr. Margery S. Foster came to Hollins early in 1964 after six years spent at Mount Holyoke as assistant to the president and secretary of the college. The new dean, native of Boston, had worked in the actuarial department of a Boston insurance company after her graduation from Wellesley in 1934, but joined the navy in 1942 and spent the war years training WAVES at home and abroad. She returned to Wellesley as deputy comptroller in 1946, and went from there to Harvard, where she was named lecturer in economics in 1955. Her economic history of Harvard during the Puritan period, written for the Ph.D. which she received from Radcliffe in 1958, was published under the title *Out of Smalle Beginnings.* . . .

While at Hollins, Dean Foster was appointed to the national committee of the College Entrance Examination Board, and also served on the educational development committee of the American Association of University Women. Her major contributions to Hollins itself lay in the total reorganization of the calendar and the curriculum and in the establishment of more scholarships. She will also long be remembered for her energetic driving of fast cars and her espousal of moonlit climbs up Tinker.

In January 1967, Dean Foster resigned from Hollins, moving on to assume the post of dean at Douglass College.

DEAN JOHN P. WHEELER, JR. (Fig. 267) The "lively young Southern gentleman" welcomed by the *Columns* in the fall of 1955 came prepared with B.S. and M.S. degrees from Florida State, a Ph.D. from Syracuse, service in the air force, a commission in the naval reserve, and three years' teaching at Middlebury College. At Hollins, Dr. Wheeler, soon known as "Jake" to all, combined the teaching of politics with administrative work. From 1959 to 1964 he held the new post of dean of the faculty, and from 1967 on served as dean of the college.

Meanwhile he tried running for political office and established himself as an authority on state constitutions. Much of his work was done for the National Municipal League, for which he directed projects, wrote manuals, and served on various commissions. Although a 1968 referendum defeated the Maryland constitutional revision, the league published the Wheeler study of it: *Magnificent Failure.* In 1971 Dean Wheeler was elected to the league's governing council.

Jake Wheeler was also active in various other capacities, notably as visiting professor to the University of the West Indies under a Fulbright appointment in 1964–65' and as gatherer of data on Jamaican parliamentary elections in 1967. Not only did the whole Wheeler family became familiar with Trinidad, but some of Hollins's best students then began to come from there.

In the Hollins community, Jake and Trudy Wheeler are most familiarly admired for the hospitality they dispense at big parties in their succession of big houses.

268. William Golding at Literary Festival

WRITERS-IN-RESIDENCE AND VISITING PROFESSORS (Figs. 268–271) Writers brought to Hollins to enrich the M.A. and undergraduate programs in creative writing were now established as part of the campus scene. In 1961–62 British novelist William Golding chose to spend his last year of teaching here. Succeeding years brought Howard Nemerov, William Jay Smith, Benedict Kiely, Colin Wilson, Malcolm Cowley, Shelby Foote, and Kay Boyle. Several others came for briefer visits: Robert Penn Warren, Eudora Welty, Flannery O'Connor, Andrew Lytle, Karl Shapiro, Richard Wilbur, Louise Bogan, Robert Lowell, Glenway Westcott, Vance Bourjaily, Allen Tate, and Australian poet A. D. Hope.

Visiting professors during the 1960s included, for English, George Garrett and Nicholas S. Brooke; for French, Jacques Scherer, Andrée Bruel, Béatrix Beck, and Marc Chadourne; for politics, Samuel L. Sharp and William Buchanan; for physics, A. Maurice Taylor and Noel C. Little; and for mathematics, Atherton H. Sprague. Artists-in-residence included playwright Arnold Weinstein, dancers Katherine Litz and Haruki Fujimoto, organist Arthur Poister, and pianist-composer Hermann Reutter.

269. Katherine Litz holding master class

270. Organist Arthur Poister

271. Malcolm Cowley speaking to Alumnae College, 1970

272. Professors Scott and Wilson, Phi Beta Kappa

PHI BETA KAPPA (Fig. 272) The long-hoped-for chapter of Phi Beta Kappa became a reality on February 20, 1962, with the installation at Hollins of Iota of Virginia, ninth chapter in the state. Dr. William C. DeVane, Dean of Yale College and President of the United Chapters of Phi Beta Kappa, presented the charter to President Logan, and then addressed the student body and delegates from other Virginia colleges on the indispensability of the liberal arts college.

Dr. Logan, President Emeritus Bessie Carter Randolph, and twelve faculty members served as the charter group for Iota. Newly elected were four students and seven alumnae, among them Hollins professors Margaret P. Scott and Rachel Wilson. Alumnae were chosen according to the prescription of the society that they be out of college at least a decade, and that they have made a significant contribution to humane sciences or to literature.

Phi Beta Kappa Visiting Scholars coming to Hollins have included classicist Moses Hadas; Chekhov scholar Ernest J. Simmons; Nobel prize winning physicist Polykarp Kusch; artist Lamar Dodd; Harvard nutrition expert Jean Mayer; and economist William C. Greenough.

273. Paul Storr urn, 1807–08

RIDGEWOOD SILVER COLLECTION (Figs. 273, 274) A notable collection of 128 examples of French and English antique silver, with an exceptional variety of types and styles, was given to Hollins by Samuel H. McVitty in 1964. The majority of the pieces had been collected by Mrs. McVitty in the 1920s, and displayed in their home, Ridgewood, in Salem.

Typically fine examples include a tea or coffee urn designed by Paul Storr, an inkstand with Waterford glass inkwells made by William Bateman, four eighteenth-century candlesticks by Joseph Hancock, and a set of four salt shells resting on tortoises, designed by Robert and William Peaston. The collection was catalogued for Hollins by alumna Mrs. Robert W. Woody, '42.

274. Peaston salt shells, 1761–62

275. Tinker House

TINKER HOUSE (Figs. 275–277) The new dormitory designed by Douglas Orr, deCossy, Winder and Associates and named for Tinker Mountain was dedicated on April 29, 1966. Its cost of $1,490,000 was met largely through a loan from the College Facilities Division of the Housing and Home Finance Agency, and it was erected by the English Construction Company.

In Tinker House, three wings with dormitory rooms for 243 students radiate from an octagonal core that contains formal parlor, informal lounges, study halls, and reception room. The modernized Georgian vocabulary of its style echoes earlier Hollins buildings: the blind arcades of Presser Hall, the polygons of the spring house and Botetourt, and the cupolas that once crowned Main and West buildings. Graduating classes of 1965, '66, and '67 also revived a tradition by giving trees for landscaping around the new dormitory. By its placement, Tinker House helps to define more clearly the quadrangle begun on back campus in the 1920s.

277. Parlor, Tinker House

276. Wings, Tinker House

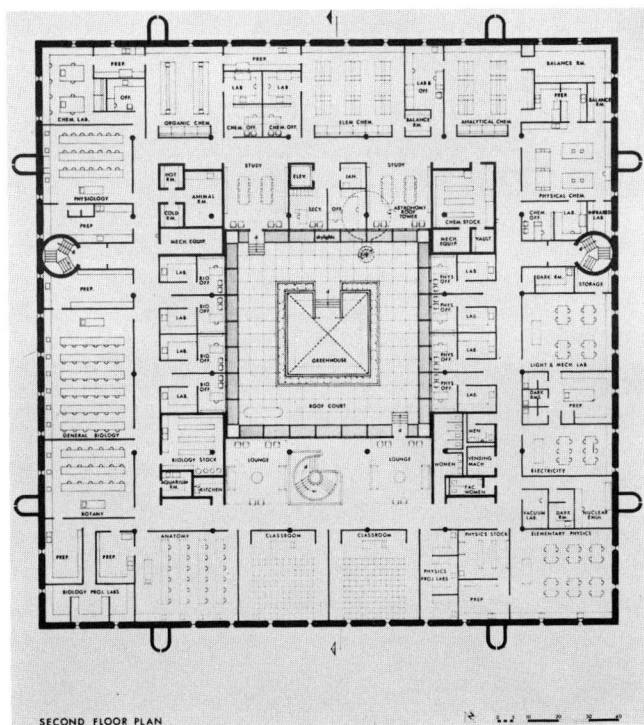

FIRST FLOOR PLAN

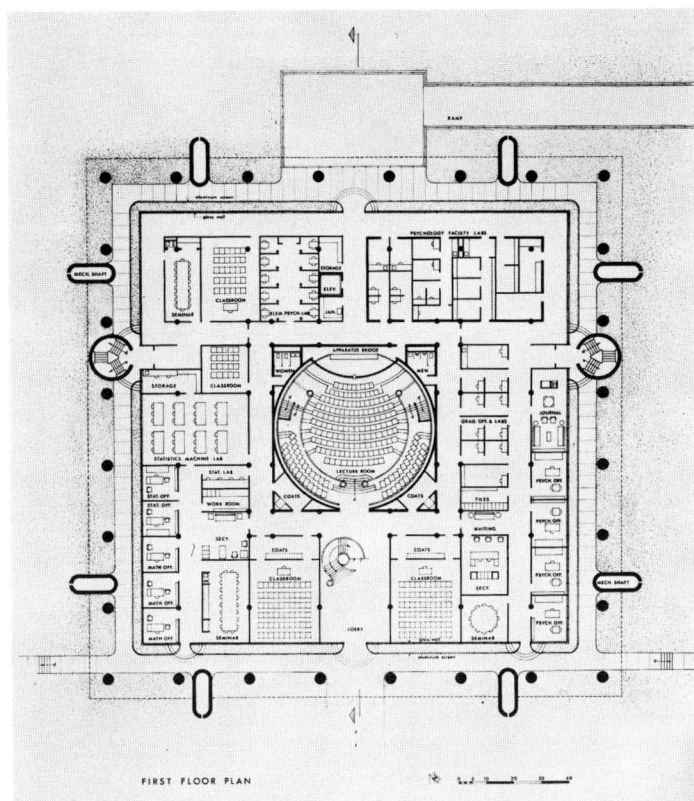

SECOND FLOOR PLAN

DANA SCIENCE BUILDING (Figs. 278–282) Ground was broken for the new science building by Professor Paul Patterson and Board Chairman Cyrus R. Osborn in a symbolic ceremony held on May 1, 1965. The dedication of the completed building came on October 27, 1967, with addresses by Professor Jerrold R. Zacharias of M.I.T. and the Honorable Mills E. Godwin, Governor of Virginia. For the occasion an exhibit of contemporary paintings from the Olsen Collection was hung throughout the structure.

In Dana, superb teaching and research facilities—lecture hall and seminar rooms, general laboratories and private ones for faculty and students, departmental libraries, an amphitheater with newest audiovisual equipment—are matched by generous, elegantly furnished lounges and a handsome entrance hall. Collaborating on the planning were the New Haven firm of Douglas Orr, deCossy, Winder and Associates, and the Roanoke firm of Randolph Frantz and John Chappelear. Construction, in fabrics and techniques new to many of their workmen, was supervised by H. A. Lucas and Sons of Roanoke.

The final cost of building and equipment, just over $3 million, was met through a grant of $475,910 made under the provisions of the Higher Education Facilities Act of 1963, another of $185,564 from the National Science Foundation, and gifts from many alumnae, parents, and friends of Hollins.

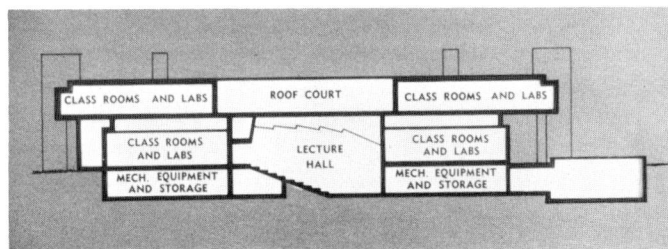

197

THE DESIGNING OF DANA (Figs. 283–285) A feature article in the *Architectural Record* (February 1970) commented that Dana Science Building "does not aggressively assert its scientific purpose, but is gracious, humane, and inviting in a manner befitting the traditions of the school." Dana's principal designer, Edwin W. deCossy, and his collaborator, John Chappelear, deserve the compliment, for they successfully solved many problems of form, scale, material, and of general harmony between Dana and Hollins's older buildings. It was agreed from the outset that a science building should be modern in fabric and style and that facilities for all departments should be housed under one roof. If a high-rise structure were not to overbalance all others on the campus, a building some eight times the size of Pleasants Building had to be extended over almost an acre of ground.

To keep Dana in harmonious scale, its size was visually minimized.

282. Lounge, Dana

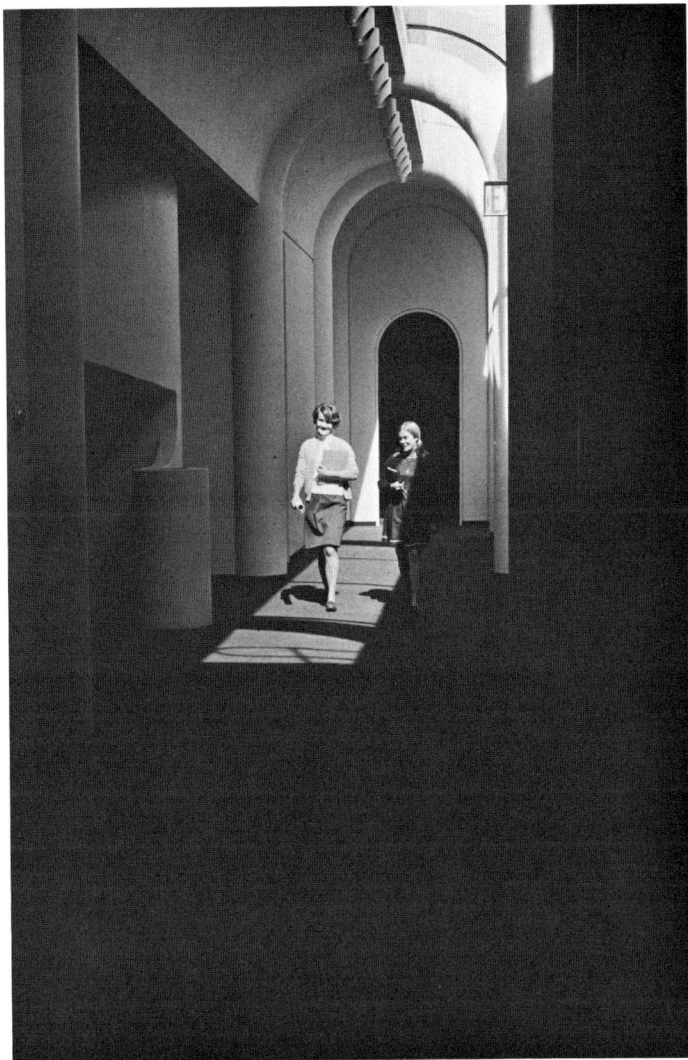

The first floor was recessed, given glass walls shielded by delicate aluminum screens, and surrounded with a contemporary version of the colonnades used in the older buildings. A rough-textured brick resembling the old handmade brick was chosen for columns and upper wall surfaces. The whole structure was kept low, with a roofline clear of projections, by housing air conditioning and mechanical service lines in vertical piers on its perimeter. The pattern of closed quadrangles that characterizes the Hollins campus was echoed not only in the general plan of Dana but also in its interior spaces. On the ground floor, high skylighted vaulted corridors completely surround the central amphitheater, and on the second floor an open-roof court, with a small conservatory and an astronomy tower, provides a pleasing oasis.

Even before it was completed, Dana received a National Award of Merit in the 1966 competition sponsored by the American Institute of Architects, the U.S. Office of Education, and the Ford Foundation's Educational Facilities Laboratories; Dana was one of 29 winners among over 250 entrants. It also won an honor award from the Virginia Chapter of the A.I.A., and a grand honor award from the same institute's southwestern section.

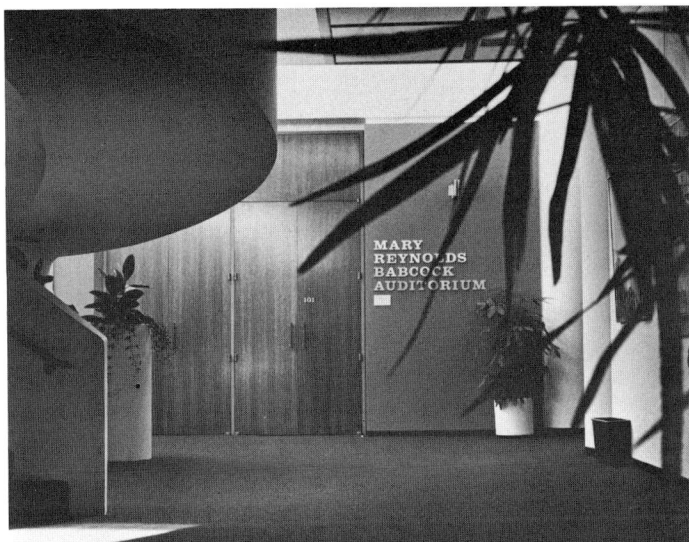

286. Entrance hall, Dana

287. Interior, Babcock Auditorium (Ezra Stoller © ESTO)

NAMED FACILITIES IN DANA (Figs. 286–288) In appreciation of a $200,000 grant from the Dana Foundation of Toledo, Ohio, the new science building was named for philanthropist Charles A. Dana at a special dedication held on October 24, 1969. Mrs. Eleanor Naylor Dana, the honored guest, was presented with a Hollins medal.

In 1960 the Mary Reynolds Babcock Foundation had granted Hollins $12,000 for purchase of learned journals in psychology and chemistry, and in 1964 contributed $100,000 toward the new science building. In appreciation of these gifts the new amphitheater was named for Mrs. Babcock.

Botany, biology, chemistry, and physics laboratories were named respectively for professors Paul Patterson, Ida Sitler, Harriett Fillinger, and Goldena Farnsworth, and the roof court for Mary Louise Mayo Freitag, Hollins '29. A mathematics seminar room was named for Jacqueline Smith Hall, Hollins '66, and a psychology seminar room for the Sigma Xi Club. A mathematics office was dedicated to the memory of Dorothy Packham Mears in acknowledgement of a gift from her husband, C. Emmerick Mears, and her daughter, Dorothy Mears Ward, Hollins '46.

288. Chemistry laboratory

HOLLINS MEDALS (Figs. 289, 290) As part of the year-long celebration of Hollins's 125th anniversary, bronze medals bearing the college seal were given to women chosen because they had rendered notable service to American society at large or to Hollins College in particular.

On Founder's Day, 1967, medals were presented to Southern novelist Eudora Welty; to Frances Oldham Kelsey, federal food and drug officer who had prevented distribution of thalidomide; and to alumnae Marguerite Hearsey, long a headmistress of Abbot Academy; Katherine Tupper Marshall, actress and author; Evelyn Fishburn Shackelford James, civic leader and constant supporter of Hollins; and Mary Wells Ashworth, biographer of George Washington. Receiving medals in absentia were Jessie Ball duPont and Enid Starkie.

Women honored at the alumnae banquet of May 29, 1967, included novelist Katherine Anne Porter; presidents emeriti Sarah Gibson Blanding of Vassar and Ada Comstock Notestein of Radcliffe; and six Hollins alumnae: Sara Geer Gayle, Julia Church Gilmer, Mary Rowland Sowell Perkinson, Marion Cobbs Stuart, Imogene Young Wynne, and Billie Camp Younts—all civic leaders in their communities and active workers for Hollins.

Then at the final celebration on Founder's Day, 1968, recipients of medals included critic Marya Mannes; former ambassador Frances Elizabeth Willis; psychologist Janet Taylor Spence; President Esther Raushenbush of Sarah Lawrence; legislator and author Kathryn Haeseler Stone; and alumnae Virginia Moore, poet and historian; Mary Curtis-Verna, opera star; Mary Wood Whitehurst, benefactor to the deaf; and Leonora Alexander Orr, leader in the Philadelphia World Affairs Council as well as in many other civic activities.

289. Frances Oldham Kelsey, Marguerite Hearsey, and Ellis G. Arnall

290. Marya Mannes, Leonora A. Orr, and Esther Raushenbush

291. Short Term: Poverty Program Day Care Center

292. Short Term: urine analysis for drug detection

THE SHORT TERM (Figs. 291–294) "There will be hundreds of approaches to learning—virtually one for each Hollins student—when the college launches its first short term of independent study," reported a *Bulletin* article in January 1968, adding "the variety of topics is staggering." The variety in fact defies description or illustration; by 1971 there had been thousands of different short-term topics.

293. Short Term: study of folk art in Japan

294.   Short Term: *Twelve Characters in Search of America*

HOLLINS ABROAD (Figs. 295, 296) In the late 1960s some aspects of the Hollins Abroad program changed. No longer were there any debutantes, for a prior knowledge of French was required, and a resident French director, Madame Hélène Feydy, replaced the annual Hollins faculty supervisors. Students still attended classes at various French schools, but courses specifically for Hollins girls were now taught by some permanent and some peripatetic faculty in Paris. The summer tour was retained, but was no longer obligatory.

A Comité de Patronage for Hollins Abroad was formed in the spring of 1967, with its first chairman being André Maurois, its second Madame Hervé Alphand. Among the French scholars, diplomats, and business executives in the group were two who came to Hollins as visiting professors: Madame Béatrix Beck, laureate of the Prix Goncourt and former secretary to André Gide, and Marc Chadourne, holder of the Grand Prix de Littérature Française.

295.   Hollins Abroaders in Reid Hall

296.   Indulging in crêpes in Paris

FOUNDER'S DAY (Figs. 297, 298) Founder's Day celebrations followed for a time the pattern established in the 1950s. In 1962 philosophers Adolf Grunbaum and Abraham Kaplan were keynote speakers on the theme of "Science, Ethics, and Man." To honor the Cocke family on this 120th anniversary, an exhibit of paintings and drawings by Lelia Maria Smith Cocke was hung in the Art Annex. In 1963 a Contemporary Arts Festival brought to the campus Philip R. Adams of the Cincinnati Museum, Sophie Maslow's dance group, an exhibit of Anne Poor's paintings, Stanley McCandless to lecture on the theater, and the Birmingham String Trio, which presented an especially commissioned work by Alan Hovhaness. "The Proper Study of Mankind" was the theme in 1964, and lectures were given by Constance E. Smith, Richard Hofstadter, and Wilbert E. Moore. Then in 1965 the humanities division offered "A Look at the Middle Ages," with talks by Gaines Post, Berthe Marti, and the Reverend George A. Linbeck.

The year-long commemoration of Hollins's 125th anniversary ran from Founder's Day, 1967, with former governor Ellis G. Arnall of Georgia as speaker, to that of 1968, with music by the Juilliard String Quartet and an address by Erwin D. Canham, editor of the *Christian Science Monitor*. From then on usually the visiting Phi Beta Kappa lecturer served as keynote speaker.

297.   President Logan with lecturers Grunbaum and Kaplan

298.   Founder's Day procession, 1970

299. *New World Beasts*

LITERARY FESTIVALS (Figs. 299–302) The literary festivals inaugurated by Grapheon and the English department in 1960 became traditional in the following decade. Hollins girls served as hostesses to faculty and student visitors from other colleges who came to share in discussions, readings of student poetry, and banquets. Featured were Hollins writers-in-residence and others, among them Elizabeth Janeway, Randall Jarrell, William Styron, John Barth, James Dickey, Henry Taylor, Richard Wilbur, James Seay, E. Reed Whittemore, and A. D. Hope.

Featured also were dramatic premieres: in 1965 Arnold Weinstein's *The Party,* in 1966 William Jay Smith's *The Straw Market,* in 1967 Thomas Atkin's *New World Beasts,* and in 1969 Paula Levine's dance program, *Auto-Kinetic Configurations.*

An additional festival honoring the centennial of William Butler Yeats extended through a week in November 1965.

300. *Auto-Kinetic Configurations*

301. John Barth and Mrs. John A. Logan, Jr., at Literary Festival banquet, 1967

302. Professor John A. Allen with Henry Taylor, James Dickey, and James Seay

303. Model Security Council, 1968

MODEL SECURITY COUNCILS (Fig. 303) Model Security Councils, following procedures stipulated by the United Nations, became popular at many colleges during the 1960s. The first Hollins session, sponsored by Forum and the Philosophy and International Relations clubs, was held in April 1964. Delegates representing eleven member nations considered then the Cyprus problem and the question of the admission of Red China to the U.N.

Speakers at later sessions included figures such as Chief S. O. Adebo, Nigerian representative to the U.N., in 1967, and Dr. John G. Stoessinger, director of the U.N.'s division of political affairs, in 1971.

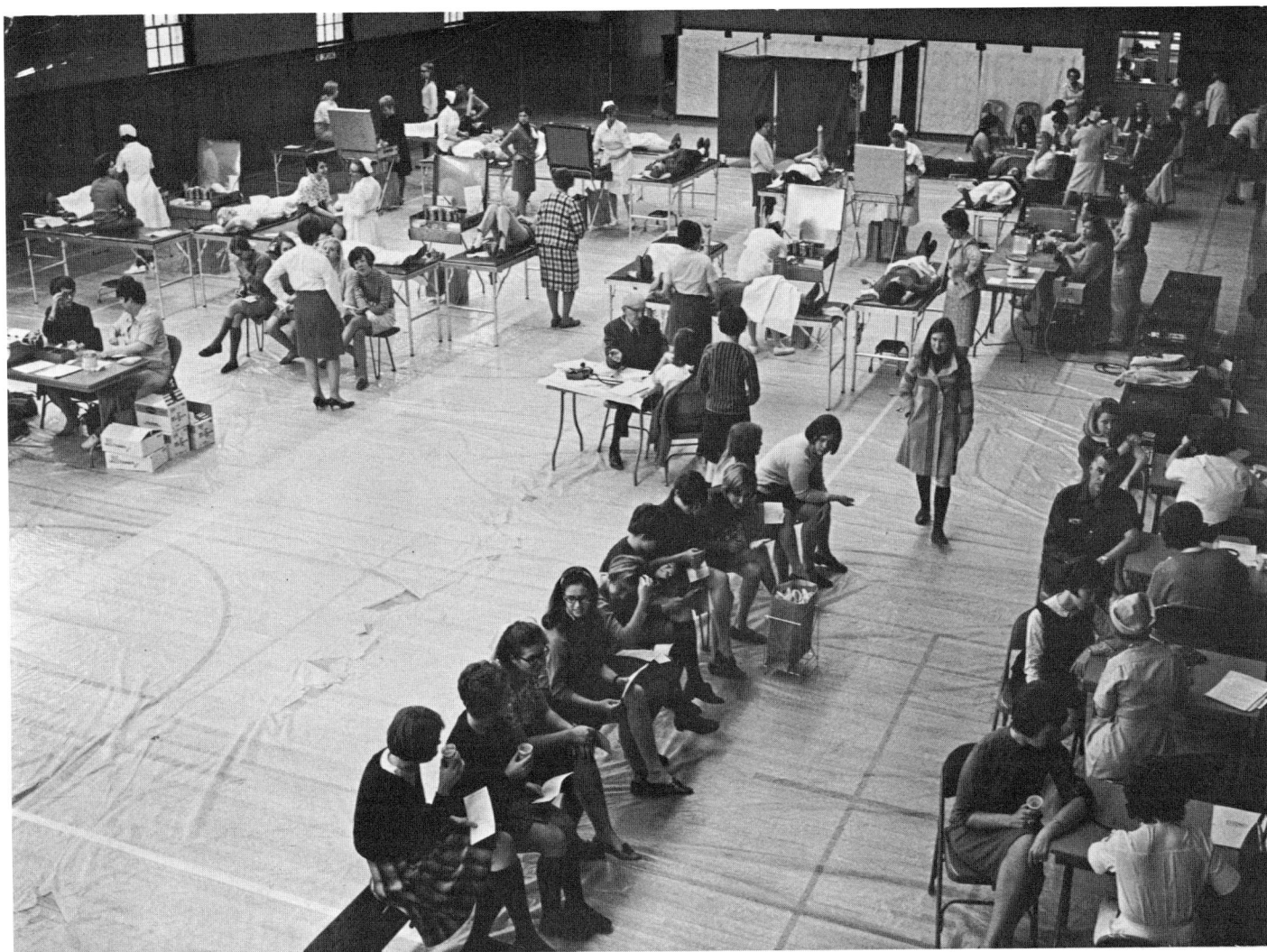

RELIGIOUS LIFE ASSOCIATION (Fig. 304) An active R.L.A. continued to offer through the 1960s a wide variety of worship programs and service projects. From 1965 on, it sponsored intercollegiate conferences as well as intramural study programs focused on general student concerns. In the words of a pamphlet on religious life, "highly controversial speakers on black power, student protests, women's liberation, and the drug culture have been brought to campus. . . . Marxism and magic, abortion and revolution are analyzed and criticized." White Gift monetary contributions were made in 1971 to Planned-Parenthood World Population, to the American Mental Health Foundation, and to Trust, the Roanoke Valley Student Trouble Center. For weekend recreation, R.L.A. provided the coffeehouse, "Purgatory," in duPont Chapel's basement.

R.L.A. also organized the visits of the Red Cross bloodmobile, for which Tayloe Gymnasium assumed a new function. In 1968 students, faculty, and staff contributed blood so generously that Hollins set a new women's college record for western Virginia.

CRISIS IN MAY, 1970 (Fig. 305) The Hollins community was keenly affected by the despair, frustration, and bitterness that swept through college campuses after four students were killed in a confrontation between antiwar demonstrators and Ohio National Guardsmen at Kent State University on May 4, 1970. Torn by emotional turmoil, Hollins students felt it unreasonable and unfair that Hollins College could not legally rise in publicly voiced protest. Resolutions passed by groups within the college were telegraphed to government leaders, but tensions multiplied. Finally, an all-campus meeting produced a resolution that attempted to meet the needs of individuals without closing the college. It expressed grave concern with the growing divisiveness in American society. It said that those students who felt compelled to engage in political activities or to devote their energies to discussion of national issues might suspend their classes. Rallies followed. Some students kept vigil day and night on the administration building steps; some went to Washington. Teach-ins were held on front campus. Emotions ran high for a long time, but mutual consideration and reason saved the community from disruption.

CREATIVE WRITING AND CINEMA CONFERENCE (Figs. 306, 307) Some fifty poets and novelists, directors and producers, literary agents and editors, critics and professors convened at Hollins in June 1970 for the first two-week-long Hollins Conference on Creative Writing and Cinema. Together with 254 students from 48 states, Canada, and the Canal Zone, they met for lectures, readings, panel discussions, and workshops. Notables such as James Dickey, Richard Wilbur, William R. Robinson, Samuel Goldwyn, Jr., Fred Wiseman, and William Manchester sat on the porches of Main, lodged in Tinker House, mingled at meals in Botetourt, watched the practically continuous film showings in Babcock and Bradley auditoriums. Literary prizes and opportunities for publication stimulated writing on campus.

306. Hollins Conference: cinema students

307. Hollins Conference: creative writers

THE BOYS RETURN (Fig. 308) The Eight College Exchange Program not only encouraged a few Hollins girls to experience the academic side of male colleges but also brought some boys to Hollins. After more than a century a dozen male undergraduates enrolled in September 1970, participating with equanimity in classes and other campus activities.

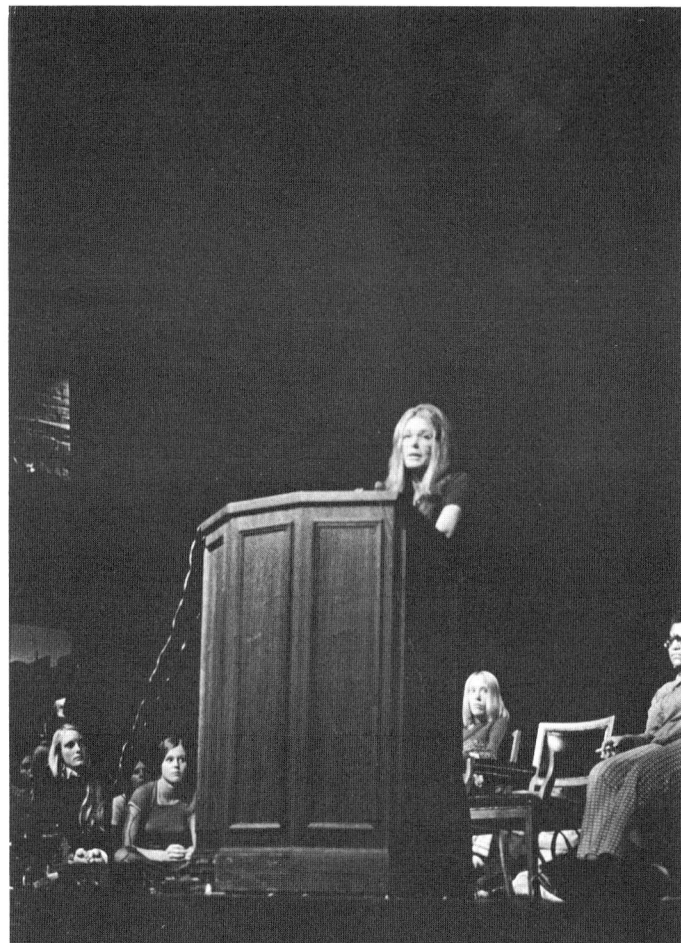

FEMINISTS AT HOLLINS (Fig. 309) The Women's Liberation Movement won many advocates at Hollins in the late 1960s. Among the several speakers from the Hollins community or from outside sources during those years, none drew more newspaper and television coverage, or a larger audience, than did Gloria Steinem. The Little Theatre overflowed. Ms. Steinem, brought to the campus by a student-faculty committee administering the General Speaker's Fund, arrived on October 12, 1971, bringing with her Dorothy Pitman; both were to speak formally and to hold conferences. Ms. Steinem, reported the *Columns,* "gave 'a whirlwind tour of history,' explaining the origins of the oppression of women and the political, social, economic, religious, and psychological reasons for its existence. Enumerating many of the ways women were oppressed, such as the marriage and abortion laws, she called for action on a political level. She also showed the analogies which could be drawn between racism and sexism."

310. Students talking to alumnae, 1971

311. Alumnae reunion, 1969

ALUMNAE COLLEGE (Figs. 310–312) The Alumnae College was revived in 1965 and scheduled for two days at commencement. Designed to offer intellectual stimulus to the alumnae, each program included business meeting, banquet, class-reunion parties, and lectures by faculty members, and usually a musical or dramatic program and art exhibit. Themes ranged from the 1965 "Contemporary Problems of the Soviet Union" to the presentation of varied aspects of American culture in the program for 1971.

312. Head table at alumnae banquet

EXPANSION TO THE SOUTH (Figs. 313–317) By 1970 the southern aspect of the campus had changed considerably. The placement of Dana Science Building gave a more central focus to the Fishburn Library and kept the total scheme of the campus better balanced. Once again the course of Carvin's Creek was changed, this time radically (in 1860 the board of Hollins Institute had appointed a committee on the creek "to take measures for the preservation of the premises from further injury"). New roads and parking lots were laid by 1970.

A new footpath with a bridge over Carvin's Creek led to recently acquired properties across the highway. A generous grant of $75,000 from Mrs. Mary Rowland Perkinson, Hollins '28, provided for the 1967 purchase of one large and several small houses on the Boxwood property. A 36-unit apartment complex built in that same year near Boxwood was bought by the college in 1968 for $575,000. Renamed the Hollins College Apartments, these provided faculty and student accommodations and Hollins's first outdoor swimming pool. In 1971 the college purchased the former McIntire estate that lay just beyond the apartments.

What many alumnae remember as hiking and picnic areas—the Trout farm and Happy Valley—by now were converted into a large community of private homes, many occupied by Hollins faculty members.

313. View from southwest in 1951

314. View from southwest in 1971

315. Moving Carvin's Creek

316. New hockey field, 1970

317. Hollins College Apartments

TRADITIONS, 1971 (Figs. 318–324) The 1971 *Hollins Index* listed as college traditions Founder's Day, Hundredth Night, Parents' Weekend, Tinker Day, Golden Rule and White Gift Christmas observances, and Freshman and Faculty Follies. Tinker Day remained least changed of all, except that it might come in November, for the last week in October was now a fall break. A Parents Advisory Council, formed in 1967, now cosponsored with the college the Parents' Weekend that had supplanted May Day; the last token May Court appeared in 1970. Seniors romped on Hundredth Night and freshmen and faculty presented their Follies with gusto. Fall cotillion weekends continued through the 1960s, but were lately fading. Many traditions went unmourned, but there were still many activities echoing those of past years. And as each Hollins year drew to a close, families and friends once again gathered on the old lawn of Botetourt Springs, turning finally toward West, the site of the heart of the college, to greet Hollins's newest graduates in their Oxford caps and gowns.

318. Tinker Day

319.   Freshman Follies

320.   Hundredth Night, 1971

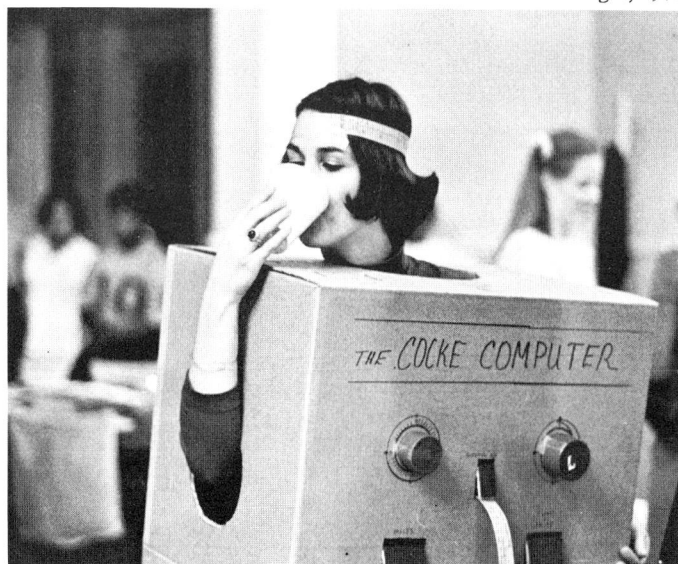

321.   Political rally, 1968

322. Campus scene, 1971

323. Singing group, Parents' Weekend, 1971

LEVAVI OCULOS

Credits

Catalogue of the Female Seminary at Botetourt Springs, 1853–54, 4; *1854–55,* 15; *Catalogue of Hollins Institute, 1856–58,* 25; *1859–60,* 30; *1861,* 31; *1883–84,* 37; *1885–86,* 35; *1889–90,* 41; *1890–91,* 52; *1891–92,* 54

Courtesy of William Chester, 179; of Randolph Frantz and John Chappelear, 279, 280; of Maureen March, 293; of Mrs. Frank Wysor, 126

S. P. B. Clement: 260

Bob Crawford: 2 (original in Hollins Collection), 3, 5, 6, 7, 21 and 22 (originals in Hollins Collection), 26, 29, 34, 43, 50, 225, 231, 236, 245, 248, 258, 271, 275, 276, 277, 284, 291, 294, 308, 310, 314, 316, 317, 318, 322, 323, 324

Harris Studio: 264

Hollins College Archives: W. W. Crawford, 223; Davis Photo, 131, 148, 152, 170, 198, 208; Department of State Photo, 222; Warren W. Gilbert, 255, 256; Walter Sanders from Black Star, 207; Underwood and Underwood, 151; Virginia State Chamber of Commerce, 165, 169, 204, 205, 206, 216, 233; Maurice E. Wright for WSLS-TV, 230; 1 (from a portrait by St. Memin, J. Ambler Johnston Collection, Richmond), 8, 9, 10, 11, 12, 13, 14, 16, 17, 18, 20, 23, 24, 28 (from Ed Beyer, *Album of Virginia,* 1855), 32, 33, 36, 42, 44, 46, 47, 48, 49, 51, 53, 55, 56, 58, 59, 61, 62, 64, 65, 67, 68, 69, 72, 73, 74, 75, 76, 77 (original in Hollins Collection), 78, 79, 80, 81, 82, 83, 84, 85, 86, 87, 88, 89, 90, 91, 92, 93, 94, 95, 97, 98, 99, 100, 101, 102, 103, 104, 105, 106, 107, 108, 110, 111, 112, 119, 120, 121, 122, 123, 124, 125, 127, 128, 130, 132, 133, 134, 135, 136, 137, 138, 139, 140, 141, 142, 143, 144, 145, 146, 147, 149, 150, 157, 158, 160, 161, 162, 163, 164, 166, 167, 172, 174, 175, 176, 177, 178, 180, 181, 182, 184, 186, 187, 188, 189, 190, 192, 193, 195, 196, 200, 201, 202, 209, 213, 215, 218, 220, 221, 224, 226, 227, 228, 229, 235, 247, 249, 250, 251, 252, 253, 254, 259, 315

Hollins College Office of Information and Publications: Deyerle Studios, 237, 242; Don Hall, 27, 266; William J. Keller, Inc., 295; Kathy Thornton, 299, 302; Ronald L. Seichrist, 185, 267, 282, 284, 285, 286, 288, 305; Roland von Essen, 234, 269, 290, 300, 306, 307, 312, 321, 326; 39, 40, 153, 154, 155, 156, 214, 217, 219, 232, 238, 239, 240, 241, 243, 244, 246, 257, 261, 262, 263, 265, 268, 270, 272, 273, 274, 278, 281, 289, 292, 296, 297, 298, 301, 303, 304, 312, 325

Katherine Rosborough Hopkins: 38, 96, 159, 171, 173, 191, 194, 197, 199, 203, 210, 211

John Kelley: 129, 168, 212, 313

Mildred McGehee: 309, 319, 320

Smithsonian Institution: 19

Spinster, 1889, 71; *1900,* 45, 57, 63, 66, 70, 116; *1902,* 60; *1911,* 117; *1912,* 115; *1913,* 109; *1920,* 113, 118; *1927,* 114

Ezra Stoller: 287